City interiors

City interiors

ANTONIO CORCUERA ARANGUIZ

monsa
publications

CITY INTERIORS
Copyright © 2005 Instituto Monsa de Ediciones, S.A

Director: Josep Mª Minguet

Monsa's art director: Louis Bou

Project: Loft Publications

Editor and text: Antonio Corcuera Aranguiz

Design: Emma Termes Parera

°INSTITUTO MONSA DE EDICIONES, S.A
Gravina 43
08930 Sant Adrià de Besòs
Barcelona
España
Tlf. + 34 93 381 00 50
Fax + 34 93 381 00 93
www.monsa.com
monsa@monsa.com

ISBN 84-96429-19-9
D.L B-28.054-2.005

Printed in Spain by Industrias Gráficas Mármol, S.L

Intro

Saying that the city has once again become the preferred habitat of humans sounds a little like stating the obvious; nevertheless, it was not long ago –only since the last century– that such a statement has become an irrefutable truth. Inevitably, people have felt a powerful and rather inexplicable attraction for the masses, modernity, technology and all the things that humans have built, so the city in this way holds our strongest desires and highest achievements, but also our toughest challenges and greatest uncertainty.

It has been calculated that in the next few years nearly 80% of humanity will live or work in the city. Motorways and high-speed trains have united towns and cities to create disperse and vast metropolises. Although it is true cities are concentrating more and more services, leisure and cultural sites, etc., and they are not just a mere accumulation of flats, it is these living spaces themselves which constitute the bulk of the urban fabric. In sociological terms, it has been said that a city is in fact the physical crystallization of the relationship between its inhabitants, therefore the residential profile –anything from small living spaces to large housing complexes– essentially determines, to a greater or lesser extent, the urban profile. For this reason, any residential project in essence contains an urban project expressed on a lesser scale.

The modern city imposes a rhythm on our lives that is reflected in our homes and in how we want them to be. Beyond its surface area, a house, as an extension of our own bodies, is and should be a mirror of our habits, customs and tastes; the entire urban space, from tiny flats to spacious lofts and single-family homes, must have a certain grandeur that its occupant can identify with. Just as the uniformity of a media-driven society searches for what's new and for style of its own, the need is similarly emerging to personalize our homes.

This book is a selection of projects of the current urban living space, from apartments designed to be refuges to diaphanous lofts conceived as places for experimentation and leisure. Apart from the variety of styles and programmatic requirements, all of them have something in common: the search for what is truly necessary from a living space. In the complex fabric and at times chaotic nature of the city, the contemporary home shies away from the superfluous and focuses on the individual and one's needs. Unique projects have been selected which reflect new ways of inhabiting and experimenting with distribution, materials, textures, and light; projects which are examples of interior micro-urbanism, of how a design can mould a space to make it personal, functional, and aesthetically pleasing. The possibilities are endless: here are a few of them.

Veen Apartment

MORIKO KIRA ARCHITECT

This apartment, located in a residential neighbourhood of picturesque brick houses from the thirties, has a broad facade facing the street. The bedrooms are set around a large central hallway and, after discarding all other possibilities, it was decided to use this central nucleus as the point of departure for redefining the interior space.

The original doors have been replaced for openings proportional in width to the bedrooms themselves, in a way which establishes a permanent relationship with the vestibule. Likewise, all the moulding and skirting boards have been eliminated, and the parquet has been replaced with a polished cement finish. This absence of detail brings a certain degree of abstraction to the living space and this forma-list strength is further enhanced by the lighting and the correct application of bright colours on the sliding doors, in the kitchen and bedroom.

By strengthening visual and spatial connections, this apartment with classic lines has been transformed into a contemporary and dynamic residence.

Location: Amsterdam, the Netherlands | **Completion Date:** 2003 | **Area:** 135 m² | **Photography:** Christian Richters

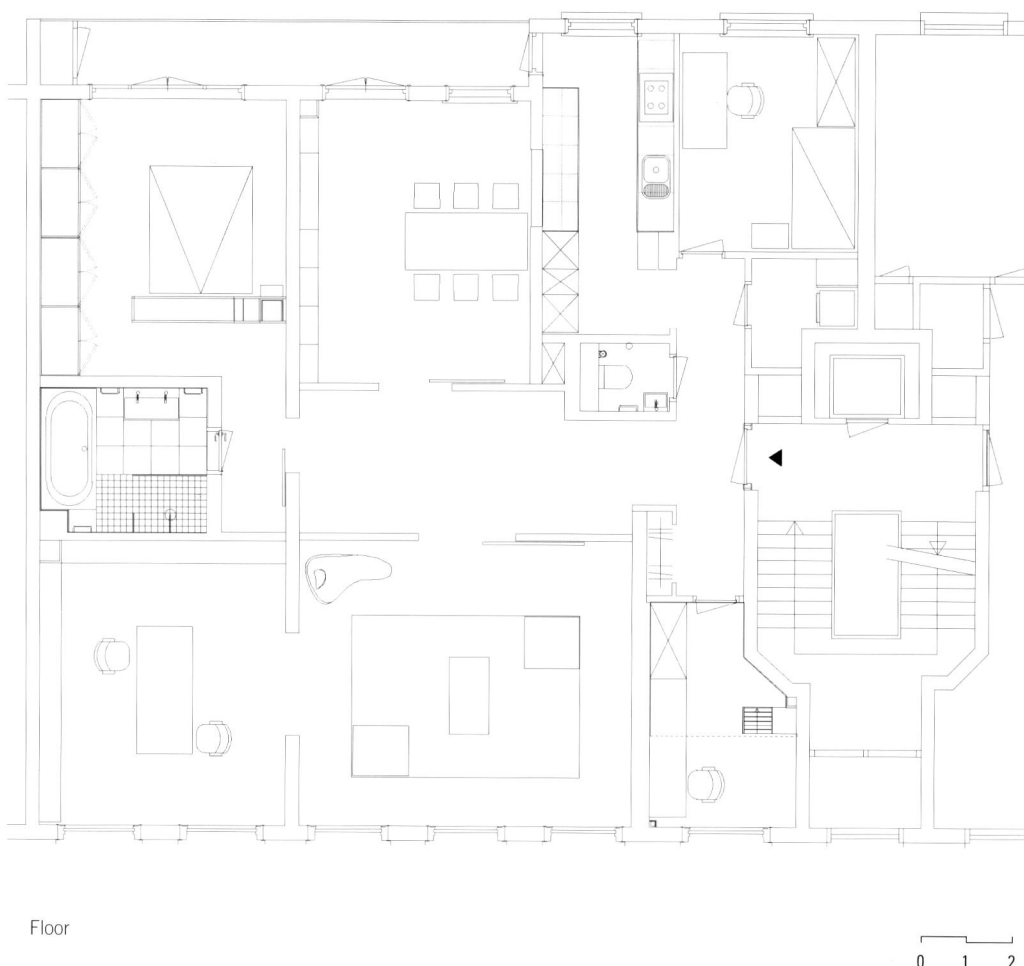

Floor

0   1   2

The doors, frames and original moulding have been eliminated in order to invigorate the space and heighten the clarity of the living space.

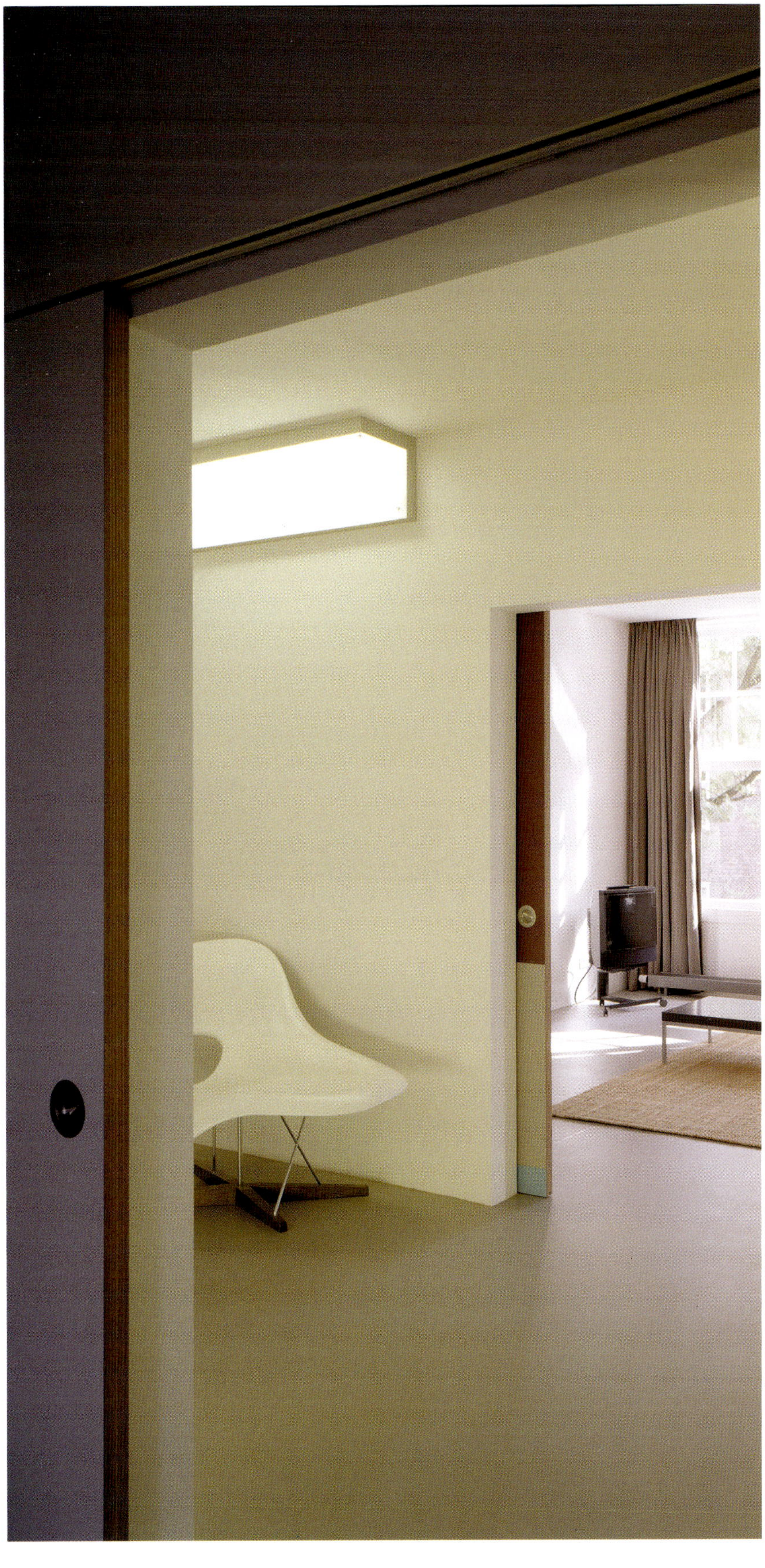

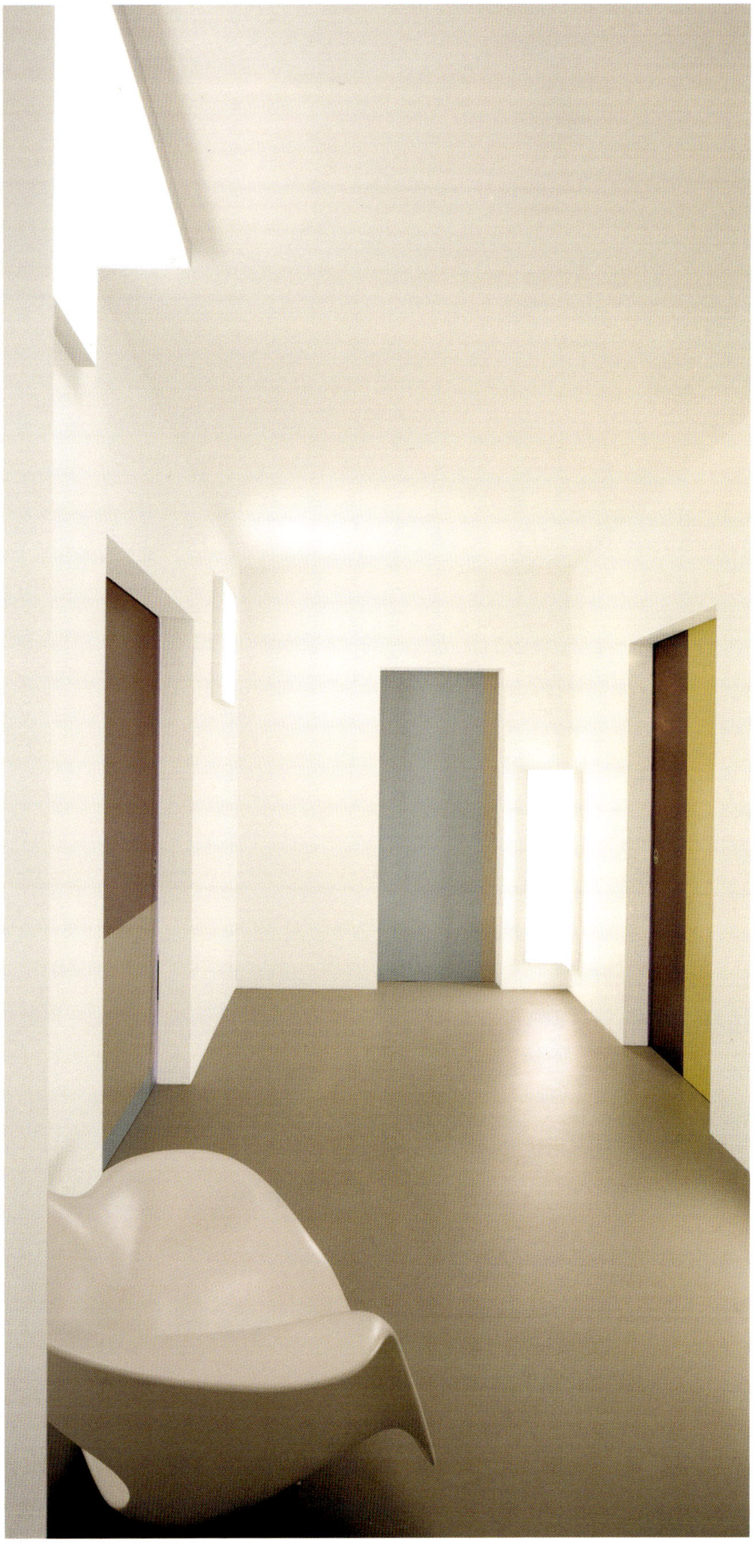

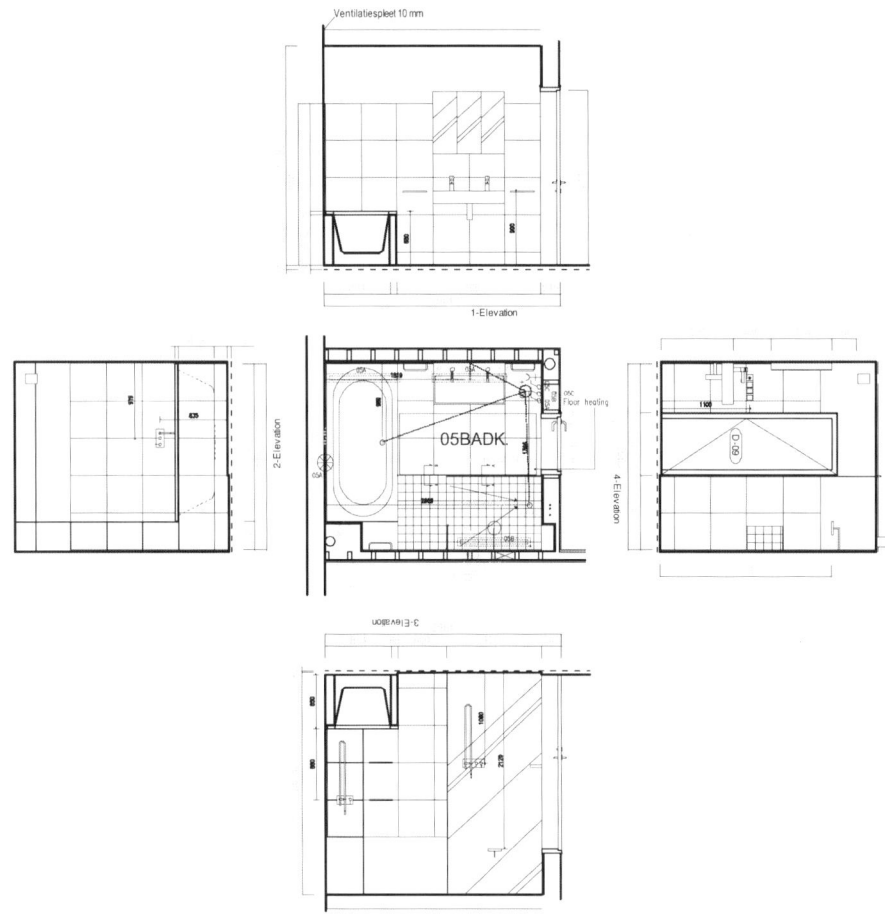

Details of the bathroom

The bathroom has been completely
reconstructed; there are prominent
elements with minimal and functional
lines that contrast with the dark tile
installed halfway up the wall.

Residential Laboratory

PETERSEN + VERWERS ARCHITECTURE

This large urban loft occupies the top floor of a former industrial factory from the twenties in the centrally located neighbourhood of Soma. In accordance with the lifestyle of the client, the design arose from the desire to attain a large, practical and quite personal space. A fundamental condition was established to ensure that the areas of the living space were flexible and could be adapted by the owner himself.

Innovative materials and modular components that would respect the client's tastes were sought; for example, the kitchen is made from laboratory furnishings in methacrylate and steel, and the bedroom is set on a platform of industrial-use metal plates. With a computer laboratory and a professional carpentry workshop, the closet and bathroom are the only conventional and easily recognizable rooms. This living space therefore acts as a toolbox for its occupant; a place for experimentation where its space constantly changes and is only defined by the use it is given.

Location: San Francisco, California, USA | **Completion Date:** 2003 | **Area:** 510 m² | **Photography:** Marion Brenner

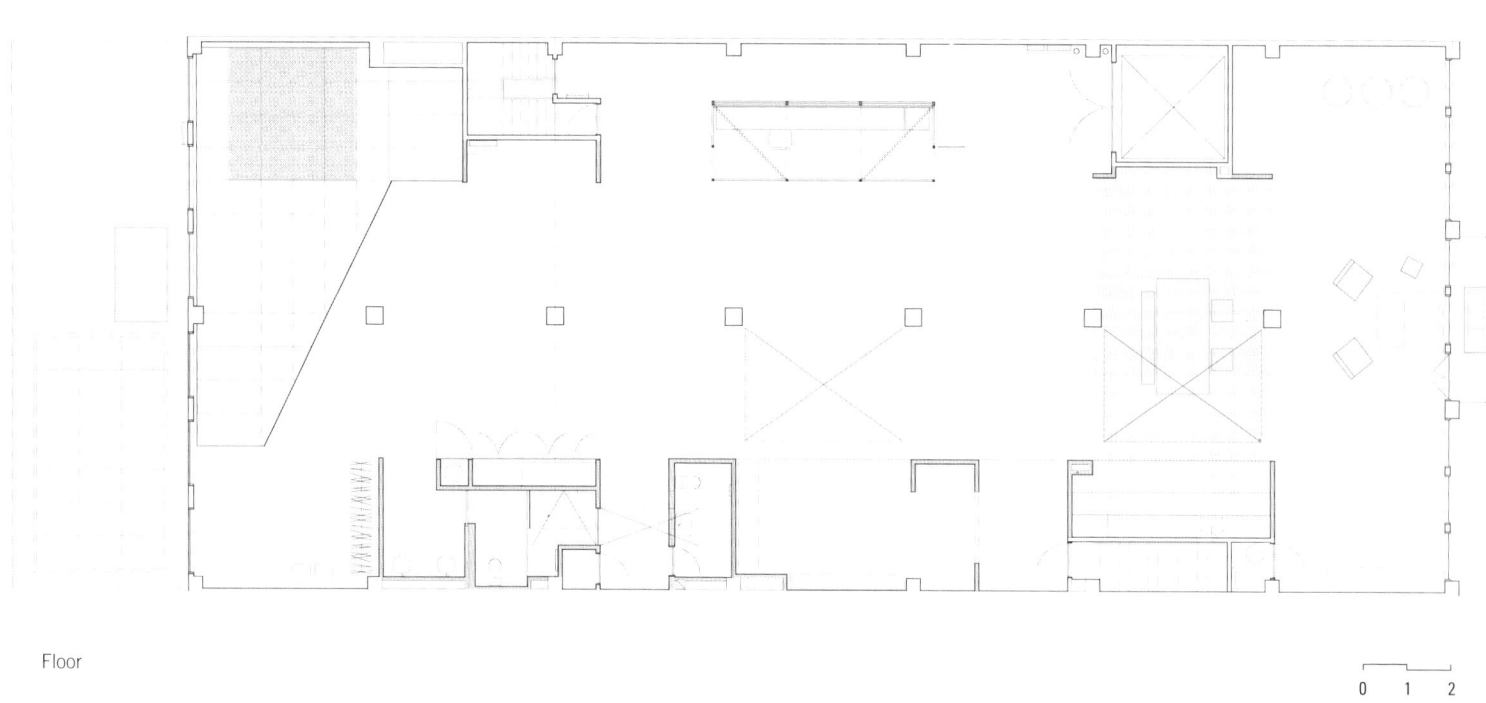

Floor

0 1 2

The design of the living space respects its
industrial heritage by maintaining the
original concrete structure and leaving its
supply system network out in the open.

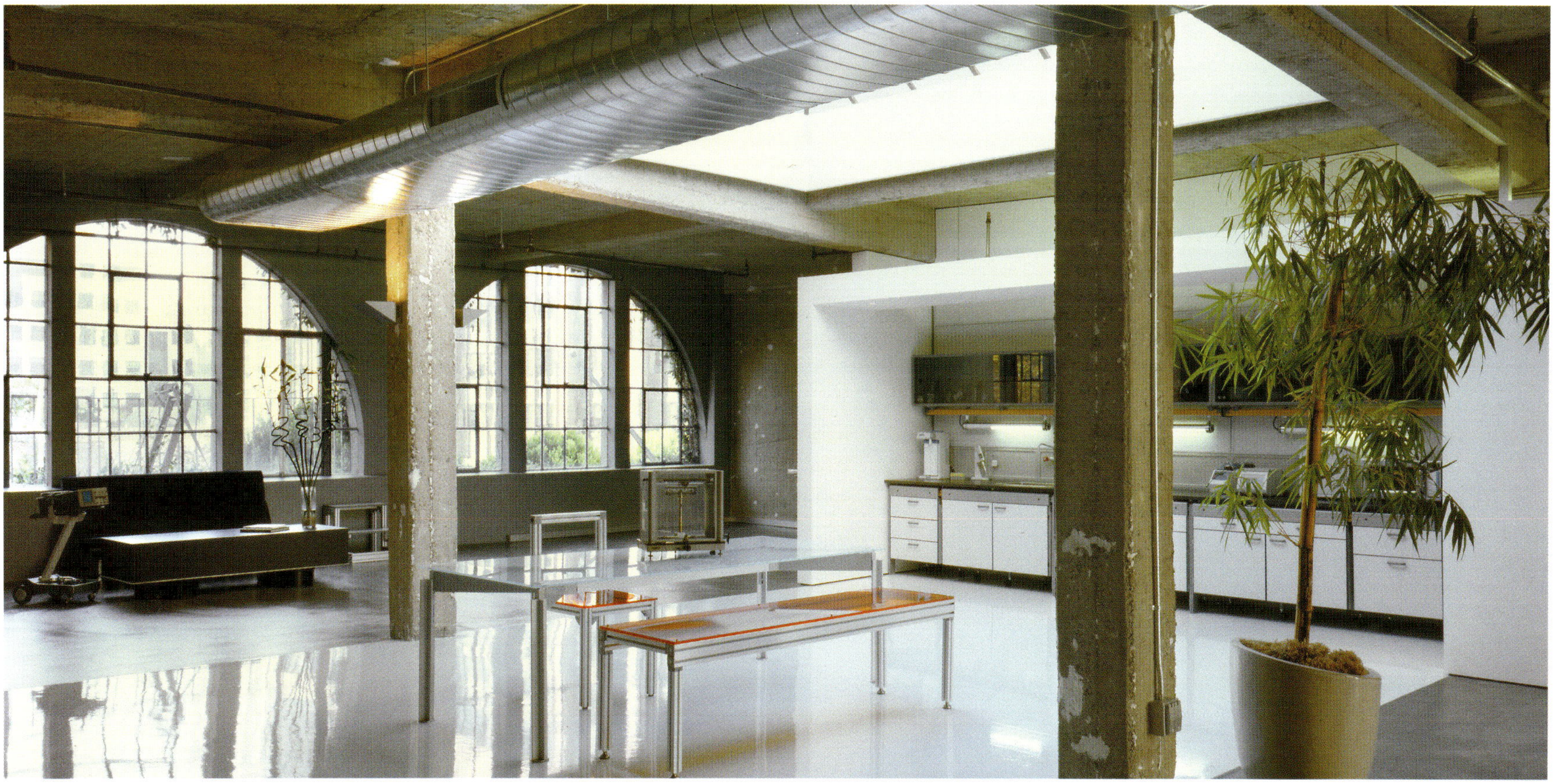

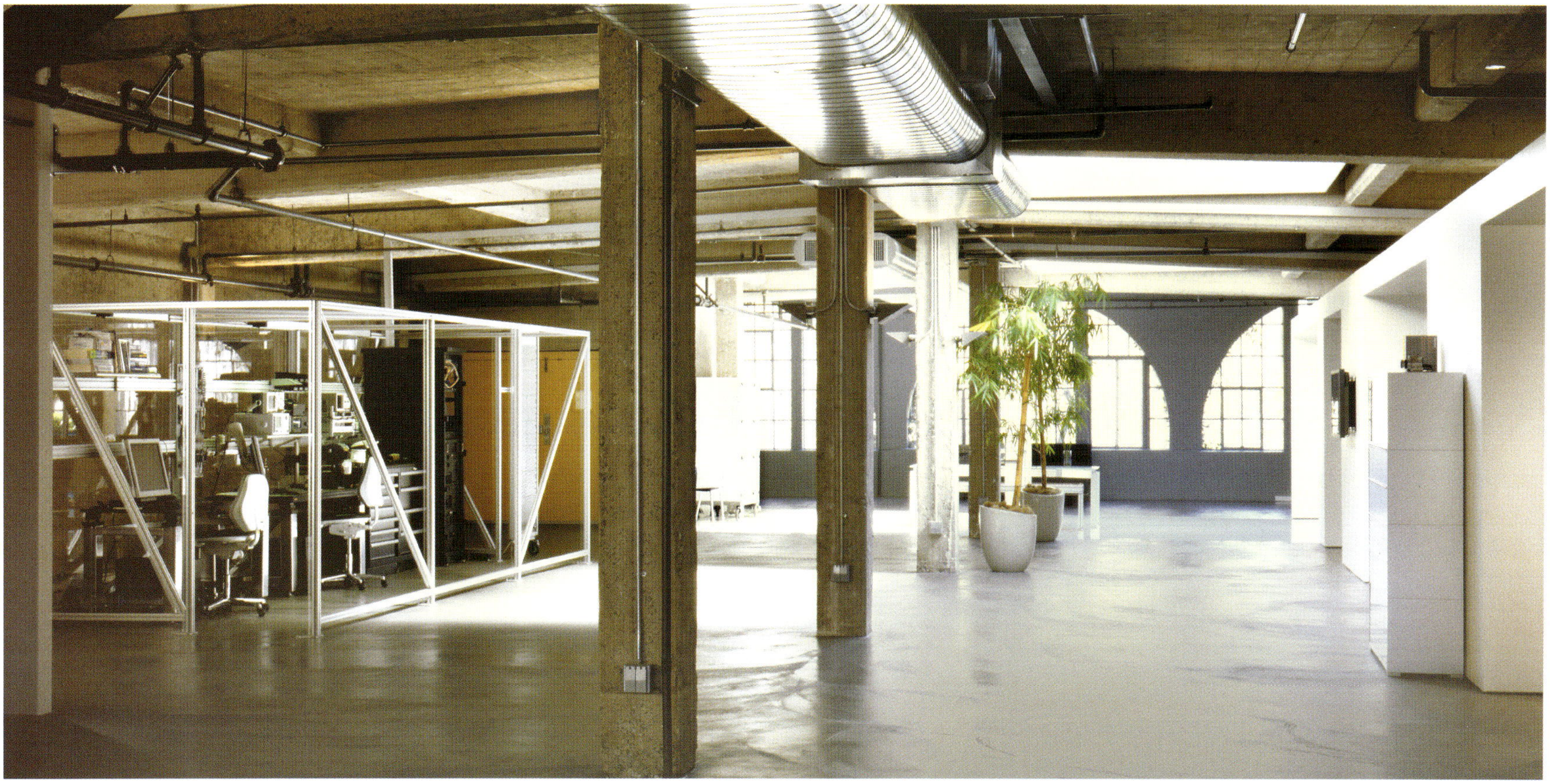

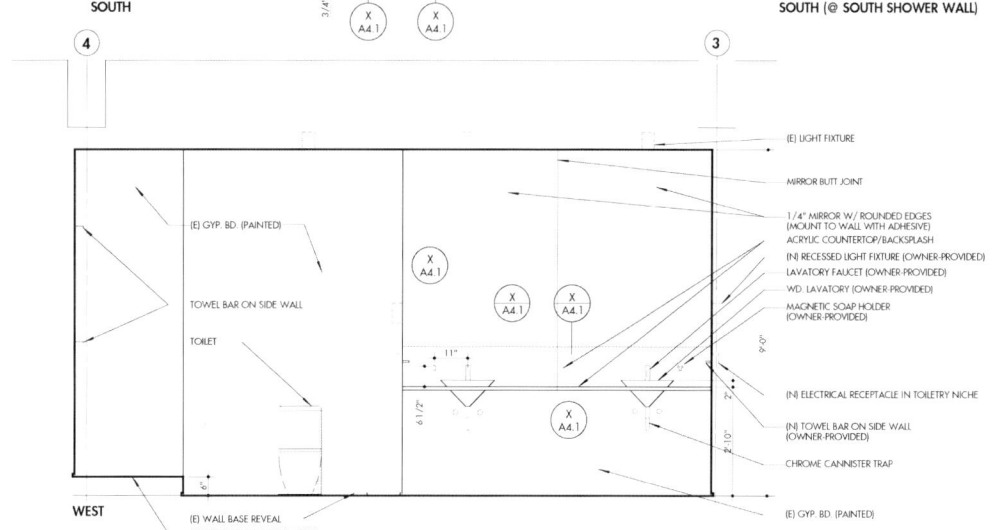

SOUTH   SOUTH (@ SOUTH SHOWER WALL)

(E) LIGHT FIXTURE

MIRROR BUTT JOINT

1/4" MIRROR W/ ROUNDED EDGES
(MOUNT TO WALL WITH ADHESIVE)
ACRYLIC COUNTERTOP/BACKSPLASH
(N) RECESSED LIGHT FIXTURE (OWNER-PROVIDED)
LAVATORY FAUCET (OWNER-PROVIDED)
WD. LAVATORY (OWNER-PROVIDED)
MAGNETIC SOAP HOLDER
(OWNER-PROVIDED)

(E) GYP. BD. (PAINTED)

TOWEL BAR ON SIDE WALL

TOILET

(N) ELECTRICAL RECEPTACLE IN TOILETRY NICHE

(N) TOWEL BAR ON SIDE WALL
(OWNER-PROVIDED)

CHROME CANNISTER TRAP

WEST

(E) GYP. BD. (PAINTED)

(E) WALL BASE REVEAL
STONE SLAB SHOWER PLATFORM

Bathroom section

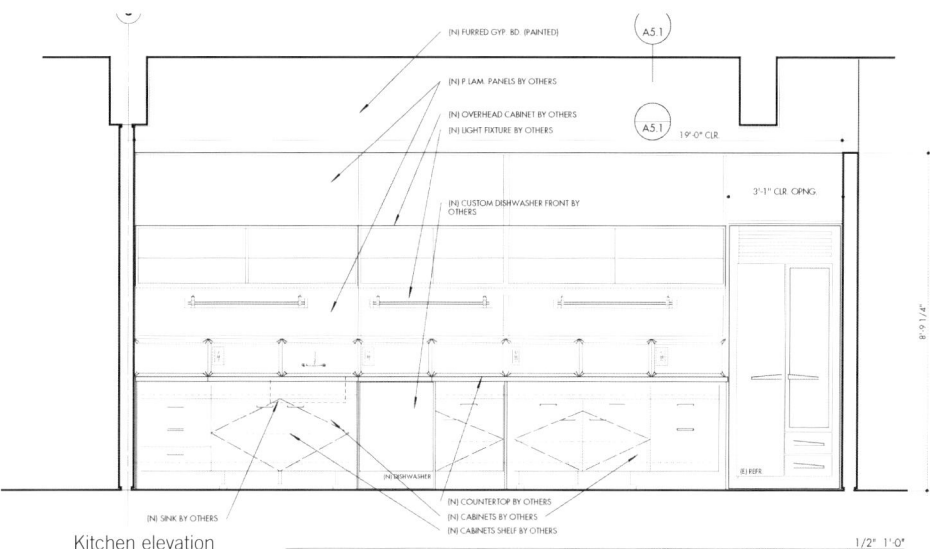

(N) FURRED GYP. BD. (PAINTED)

(N) P. LAM. PANELS BY OTHERS

(N) OVERHEAD CABINET BY OTHERS
(N) LIGHT FIXTURE BY OTHERS

(N) CUSTOM DISHWASHER FRONT BY
OTHERS

(N) SINK BY OTHERS

(N) COUNTERTOP BY OTHERS
(N) CABINETS BY OTHERS
(N) CABINETS SHELF BY OTHERS

Kitchen elevation   1/2" 1'-0"

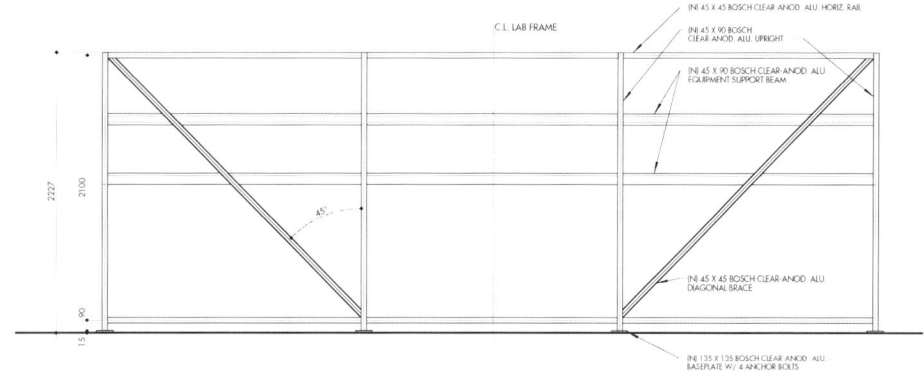

C.L. LAB FRAME

(N) 45 X 45 BOSCH CLEAR ANOD. ALU. HORIZ. RAIL

(N) 45 X 90 BOSCH
CLEAR ANOD. ALU. UPRIGHT

(N) 45 X 90 BOSCH CLEAR ANOD. ALU.
EQUIPMENT SUPPORT BEAM

(N) 45 X 45 BOSCH CLEAR ANOD. ALU.
DIAGONAL BRACE

(N) 135 X 135 BOSCH CLEAR ANOD. ALU.
BASEPLATE W/ 4 ANCHOR BOLTS

Laboratory structure elevation

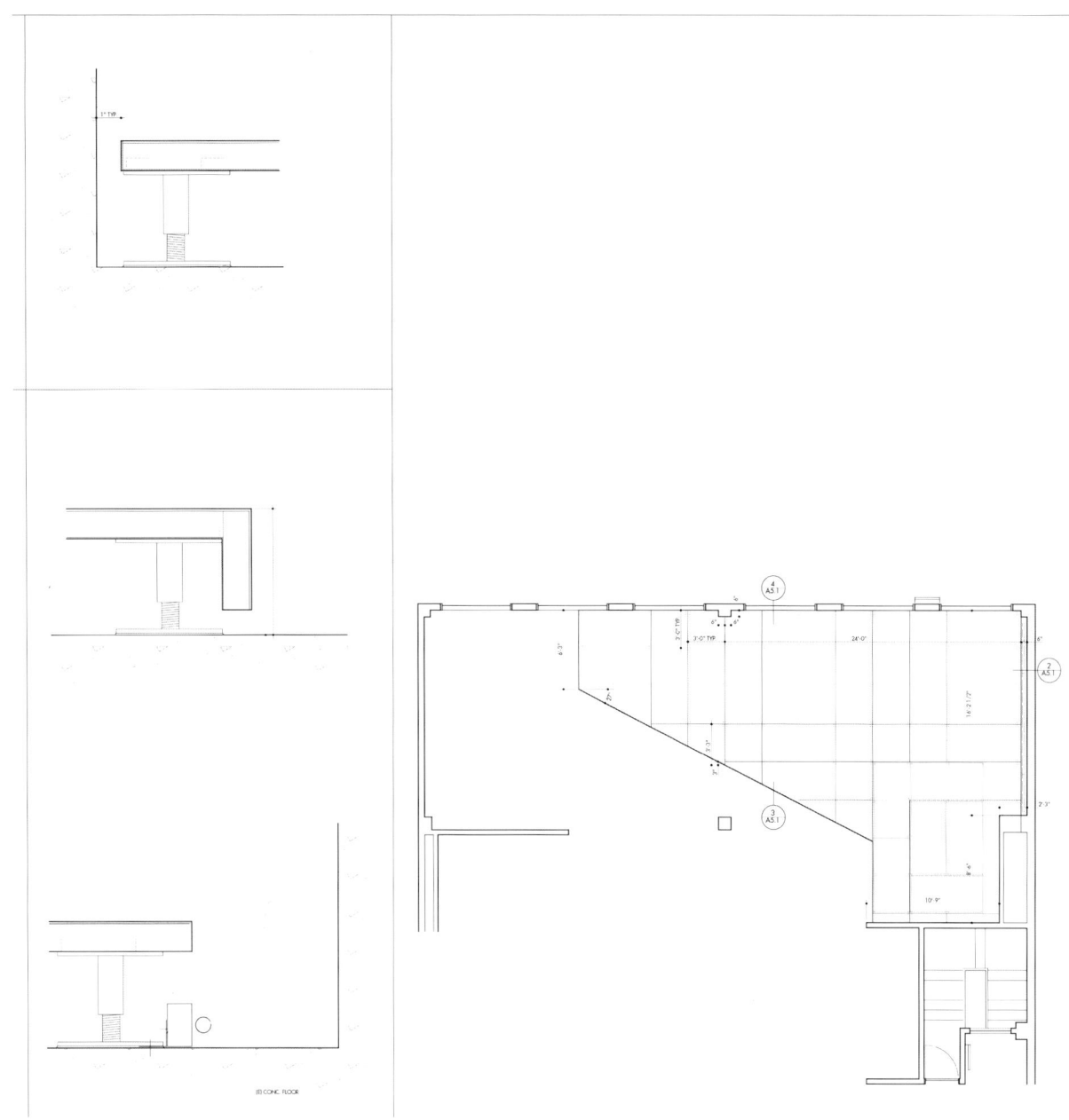

Detail of the bedroom platform

The platform where the sleeping area
has been installed is a technical floor
used in computer and industrial
installations and is conceived as a
flexible space that can also be used as
a meeting area and a lookout point.

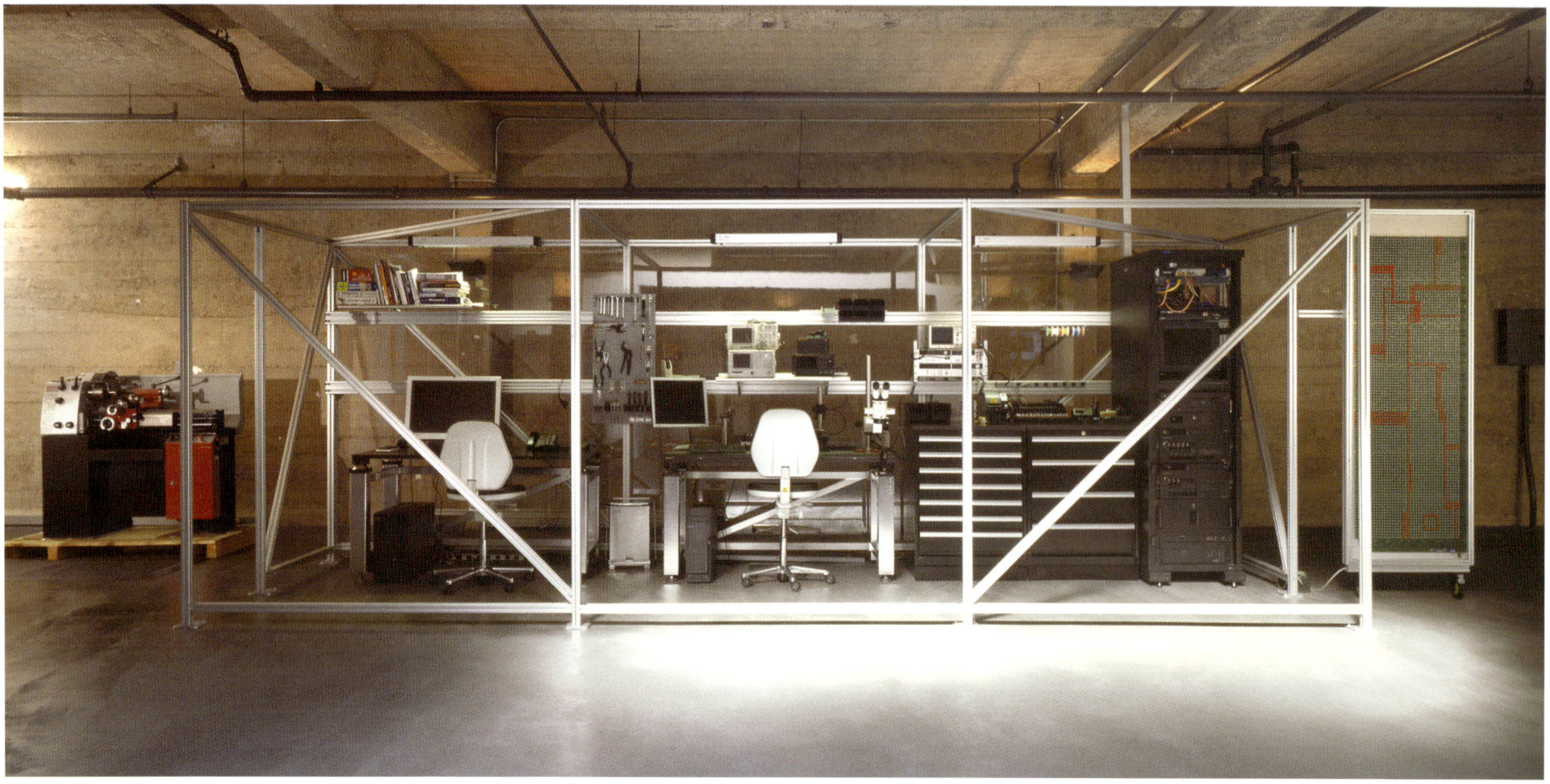

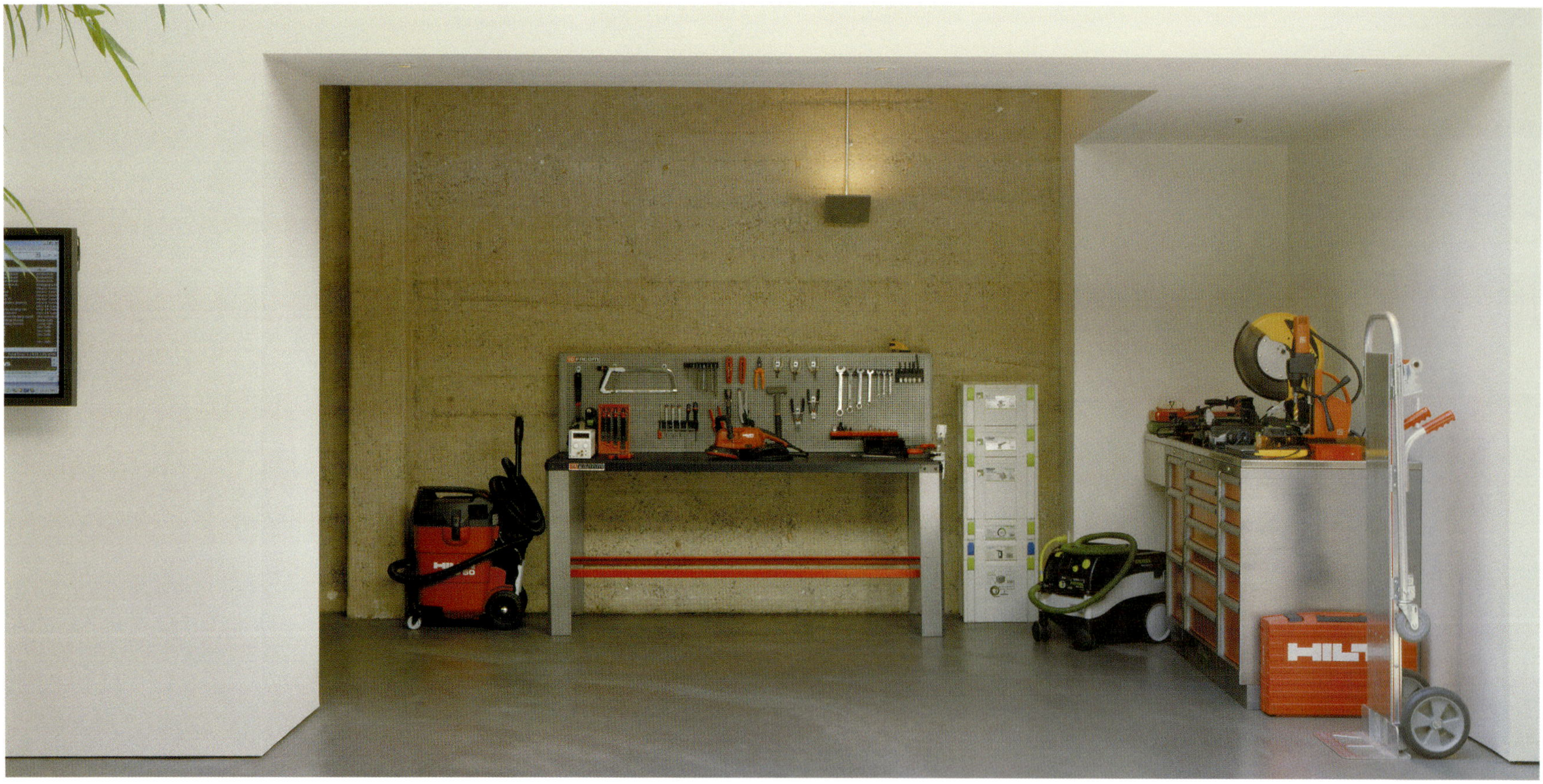

Mp3 House

MICHEL ROJKIND + SIMON HAMUI

The owner of the apartment is a young single actor, so the living space had to be both dynamic and sensual. The objective was, among others, to achieve the most breadth and clarity that would liberate the space. The distribution of rooms was relatively easy, as there were two and a half floors readily available. Frosted glass was installed in order to separate the space in a suggestive way while giving an "extroverted" feel to the house at the same time. In this way, the space of the house flows throughout the different levels with a soft transition through the open areas set off the two-floor hollow space forming the centre of the living space and visually connecting the various floors.

The finishes and details are natural and elegant, with tropical wood and limestone flooring. As an indispensable addition to the project, there are two works by Stephan Brugerman, "This is not Supposed to be Here" and "No Program", a reinterpretation of the test chart which reminds the owner that, when arriving home, that it is not necessary to act here.

Location: Mexico DF, Mexico I **Contributors:** Agustín Pereyra + Stephan Brugerman I **Completion Date:** 2002 I **Area:** 140 m² I **Photography:** Jaime Navarro

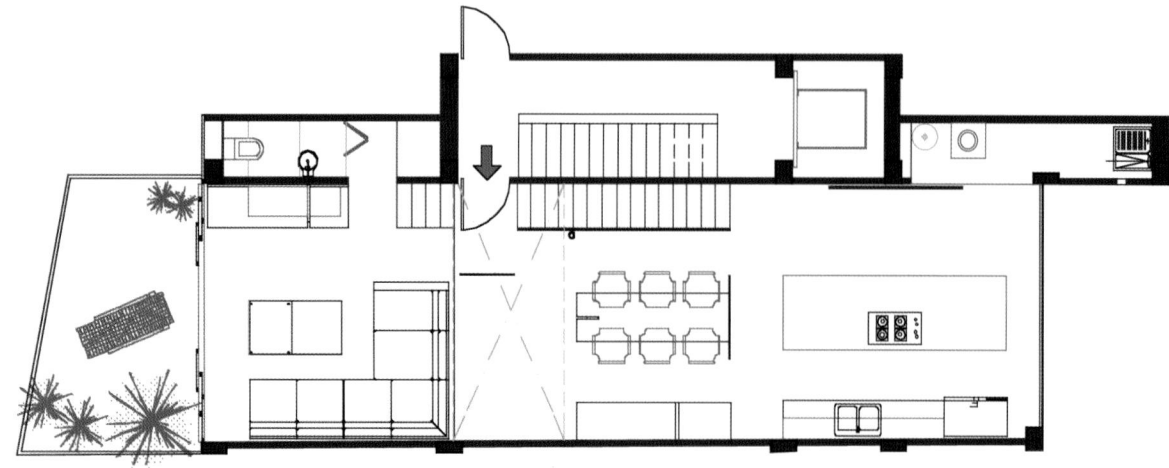

Lower level

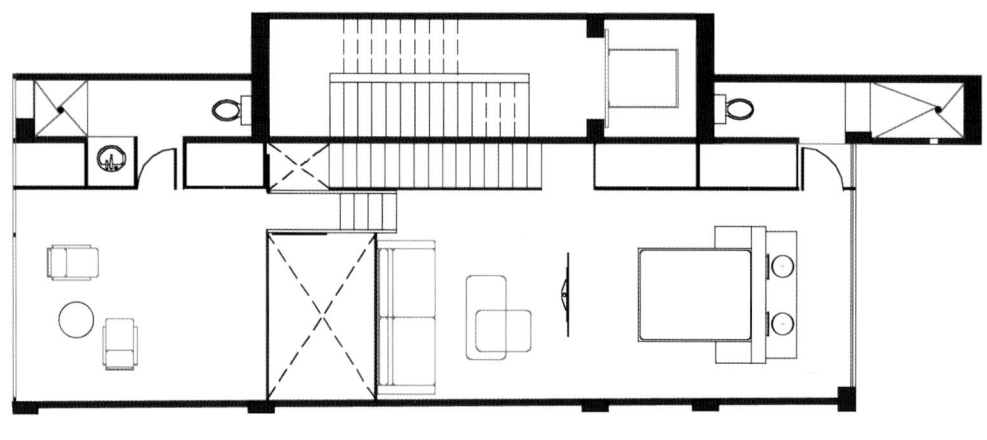

Upper level

```
┌─┐ ┌─┐ ┌─┐
0   1   2
```

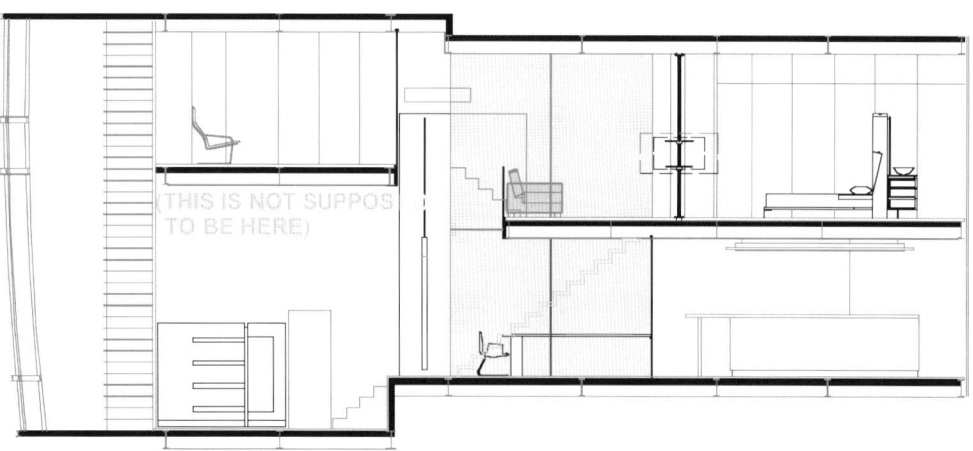

(THIS IS NOT SUPPOS
TO BE HERE)

Longitudinal section

(T
RE) SUPPOSED

The distribution of open levels
heightens the sensation of space,
visually connecting the different areas
and making the living space more
dynamic.

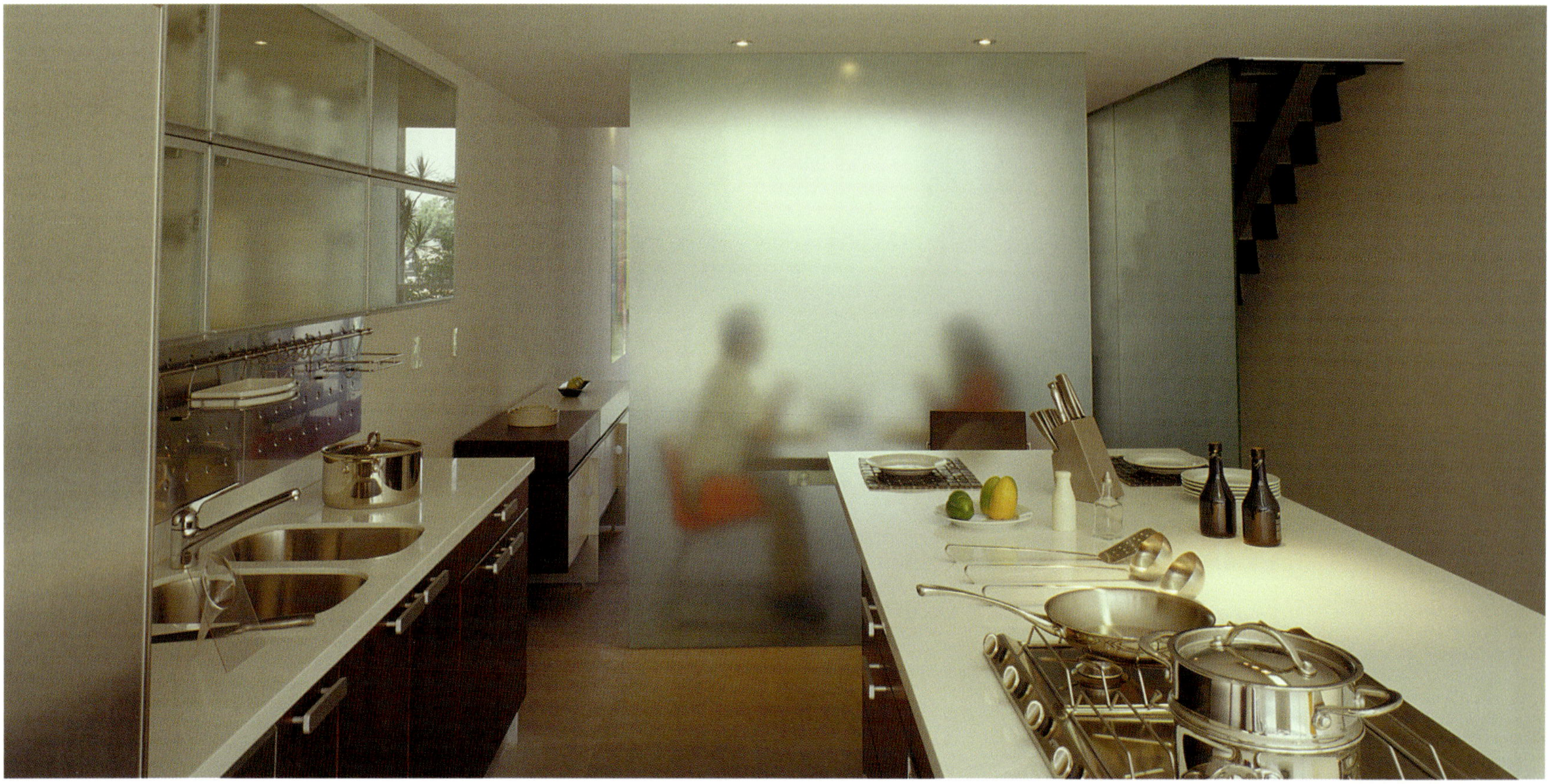

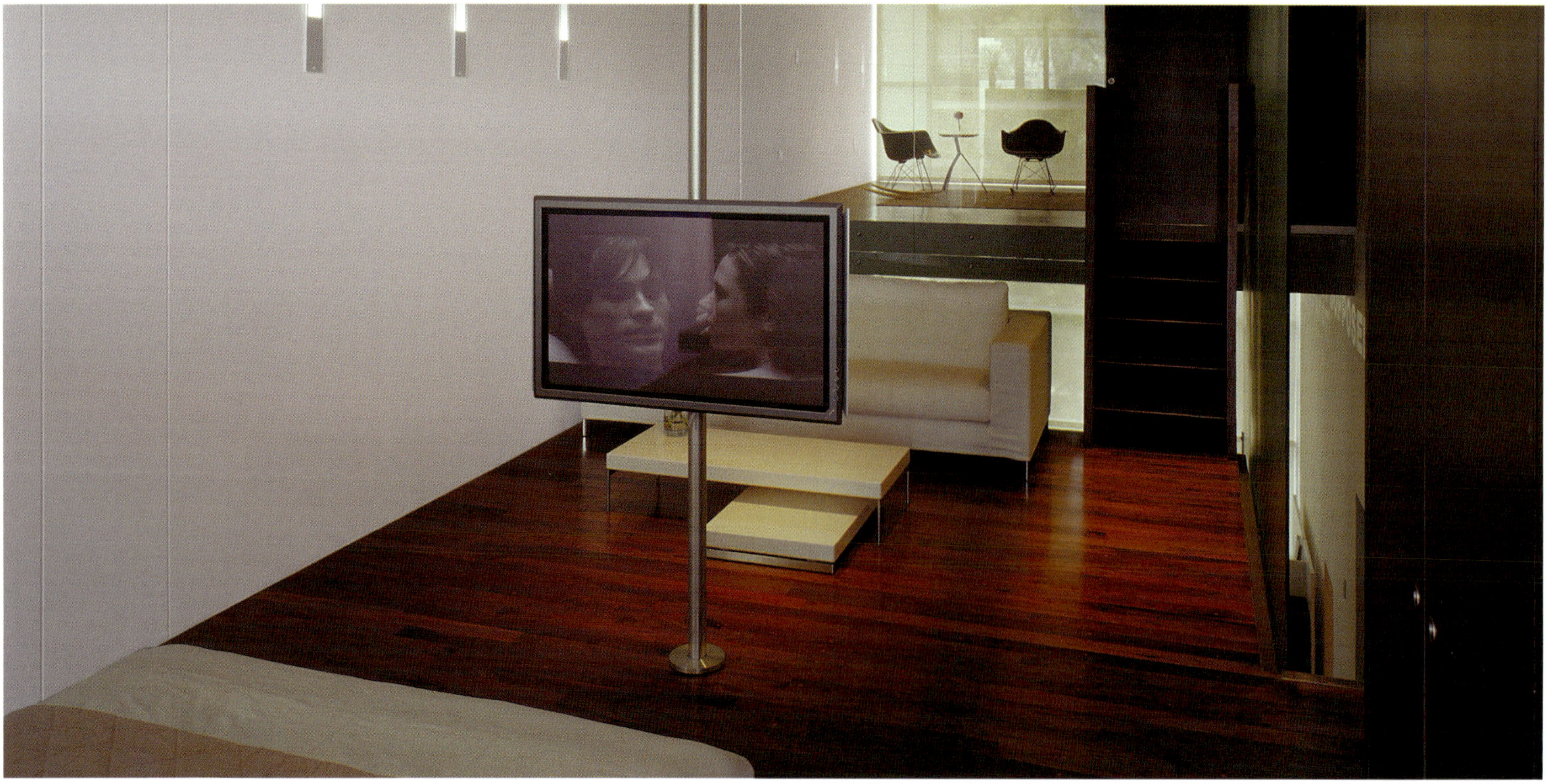

White Loft

ANTONIO BARBIERI ARCHITETTO

This flat was conceived as a single open environment, a white space, clean, clear and fluid. There is no element to close it off, nor any visual barrier, as the bedroom is the only room set apart from the rest, separated by opaque methacrylate panels (Perspex®), which rotate over an axis to filter the light and adopt various positions to establish different relationships with the rest of the space. The living room is highlighted by its minimal and select furniture that emphasises the qualities of the space. Perhaps the project's most characteristic element is the kitchen, brought to the minimalist extreme: a block sculpted in red lacquered wood that shines in the space and reflects in the resin flooring. In contrast to the pure lines of the house, the brick wall seen in the dining room is a reminder of the flat's prior appearance. The final result is an ethereal and subtle space where light has the space's most important role.

Location: London, United Kingdom | **Completion Date:** 2002 | **Area:** 100 m² | **Photography:** Coppi Barbieri Photographers, London

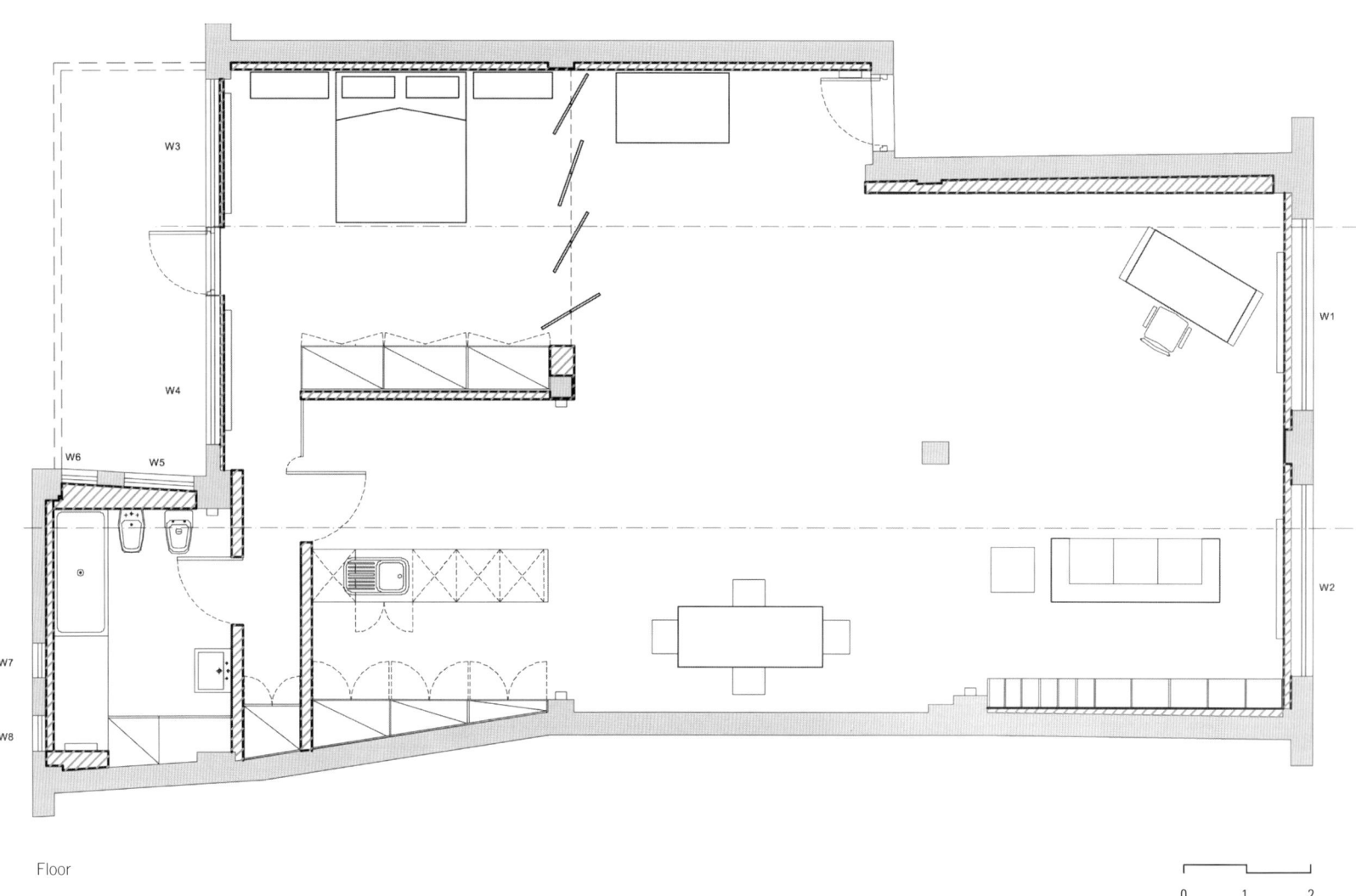

W3

W4

W6 W5

W7

W8

W1

W2

Floor

0   1   2

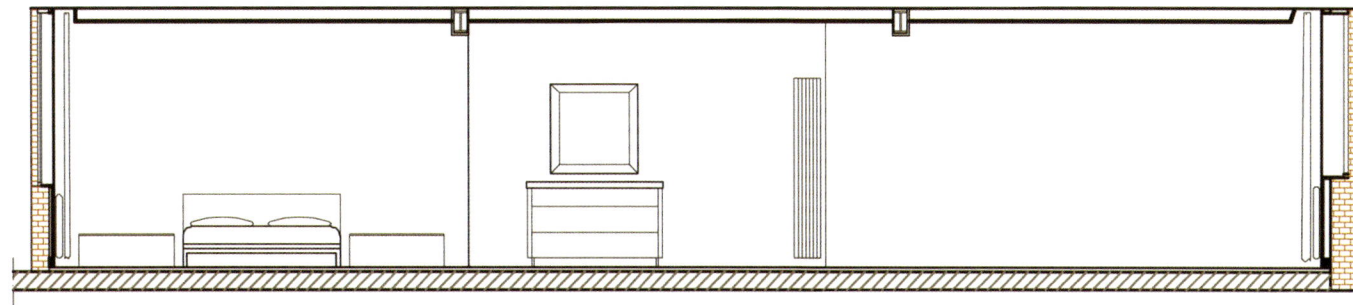

Cross section

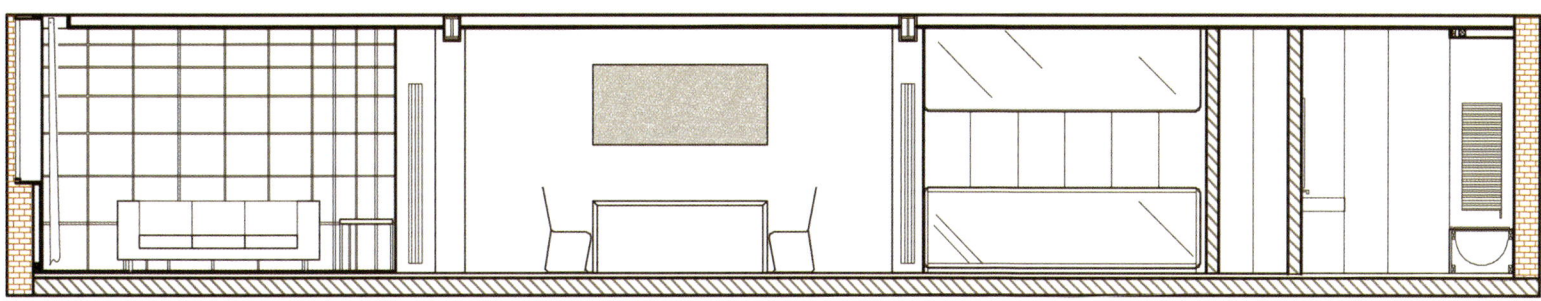

Longitudinal section

The kitchen module, designed by the architect, continues the minimalist design of the interior and contrasts with the vibrant tone of the red lacquer.

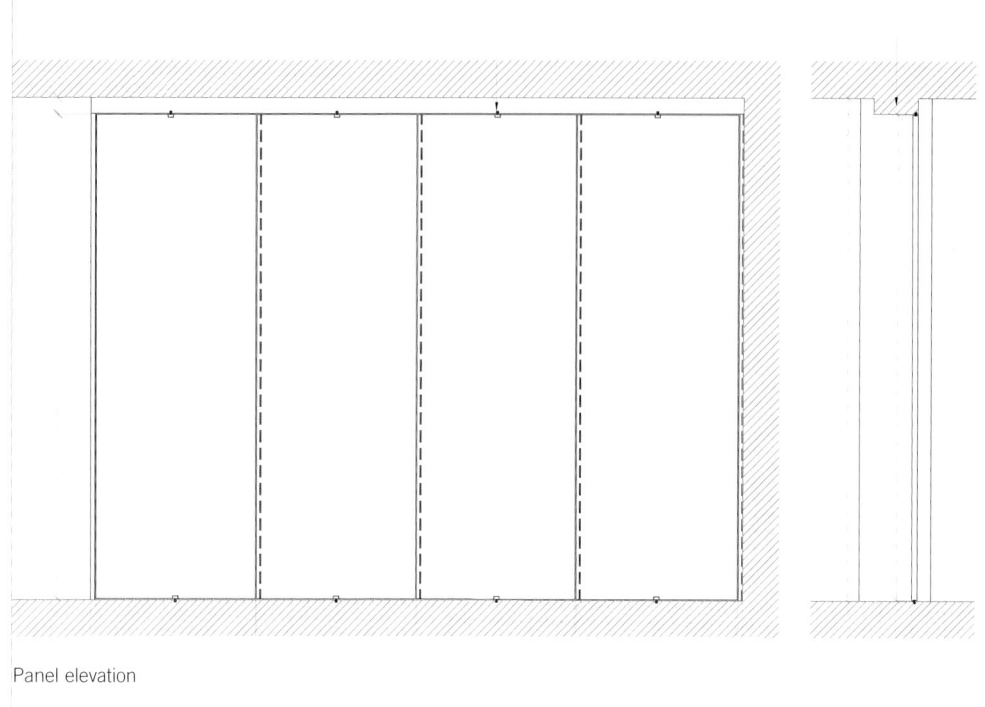

Panel elevation

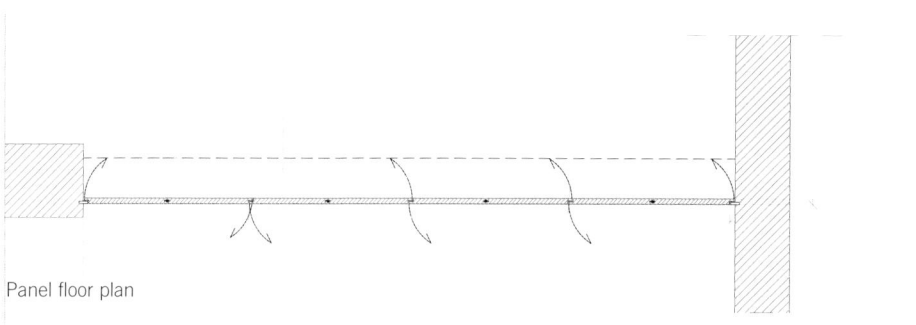

Panel floor plan

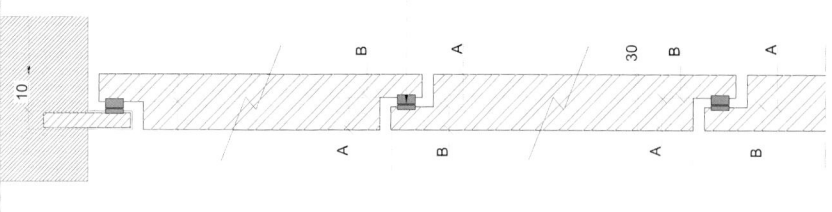

Panel details

Bedroom privacy has been assured using a system of Perspex® sliding doors that maintain the continuity of space and light existing throughout the flat.

Apartamento Jote

ANDRADE MORETTIN ARQUITETOS ASSOCIADOS

This unique living space is located in the Prudencia building which was built in the latter half of the forties by Rino Levi, a monumental figure in modern Brazilian architecture. The objective was to integrate both types of architecture and establish a direct and contemporary dialogue between them; on one hand assuring that the renovation respect the original project and on another be clear and decisive in a way that reorganizes and articulates the various areas. This has been achieved using a complex suspended structure made of steel plate and glass running the length of the distribution hall. This area, which was once limited, has become fluid and changeable, as it has panels allowing for different compositions, building relationships with the adjacent spaces. In functional terms, the new architectural element also serves as an infrastructure supporting the electrical, lighting and telephone systems as well as being a library, storage area and a place to display objects.

Location: São Paulo, Brazil | **Contributors:** José Alves | **Completion Date:** 2002 | **Area:** 450 m² | **Photography:** Nelson Kon

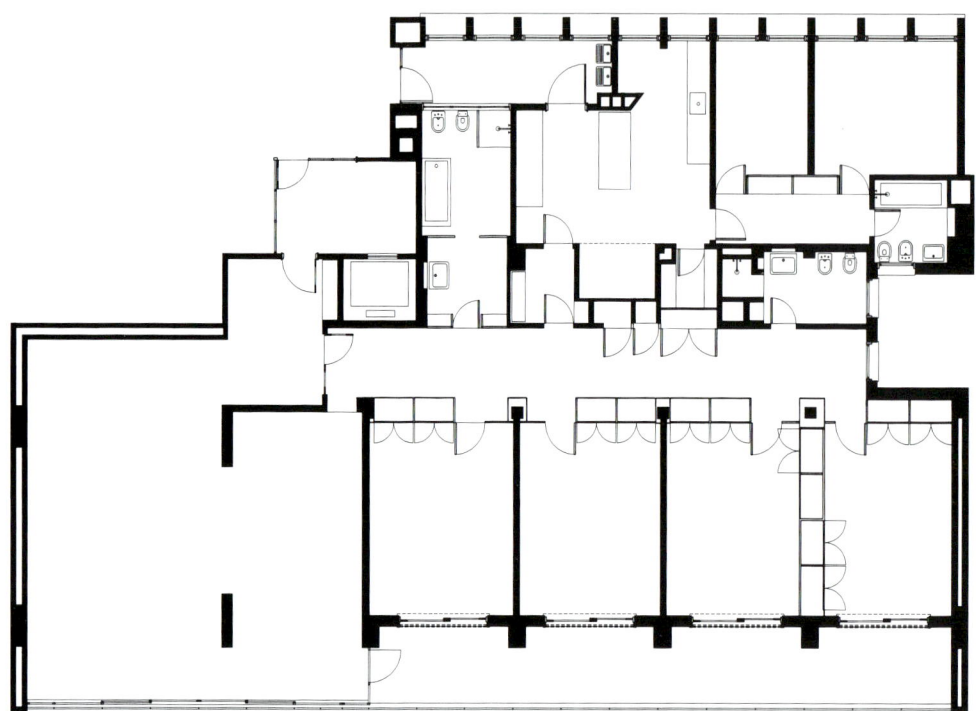

Floor plan before remodelling

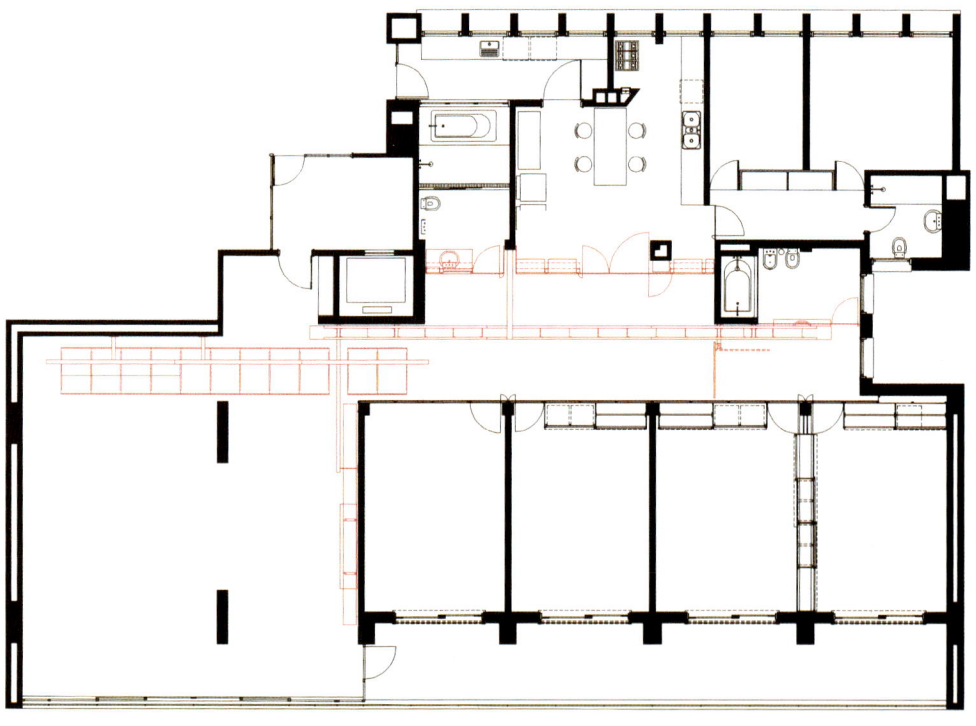

Remodelled floor plan

0   4   8

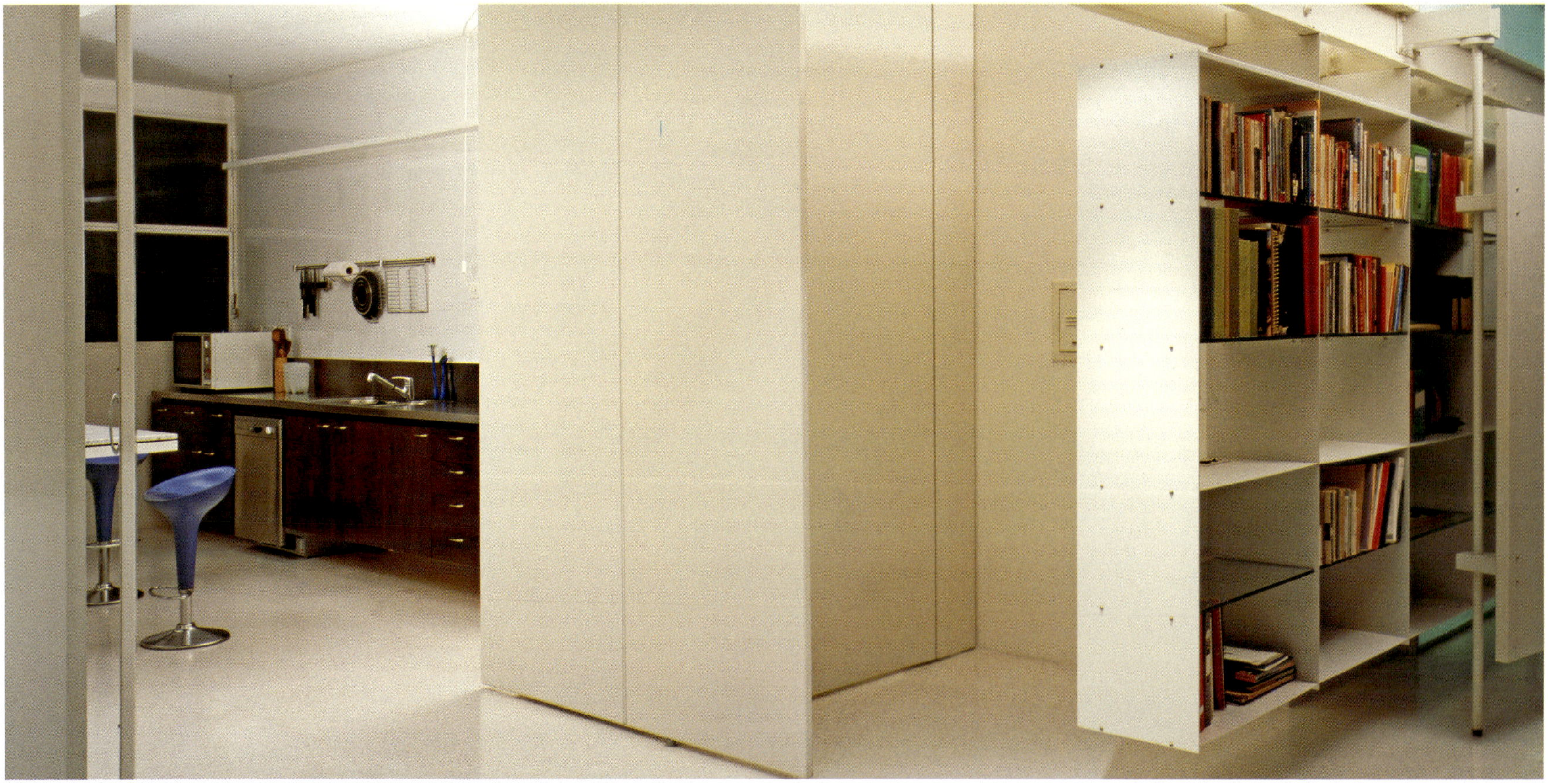

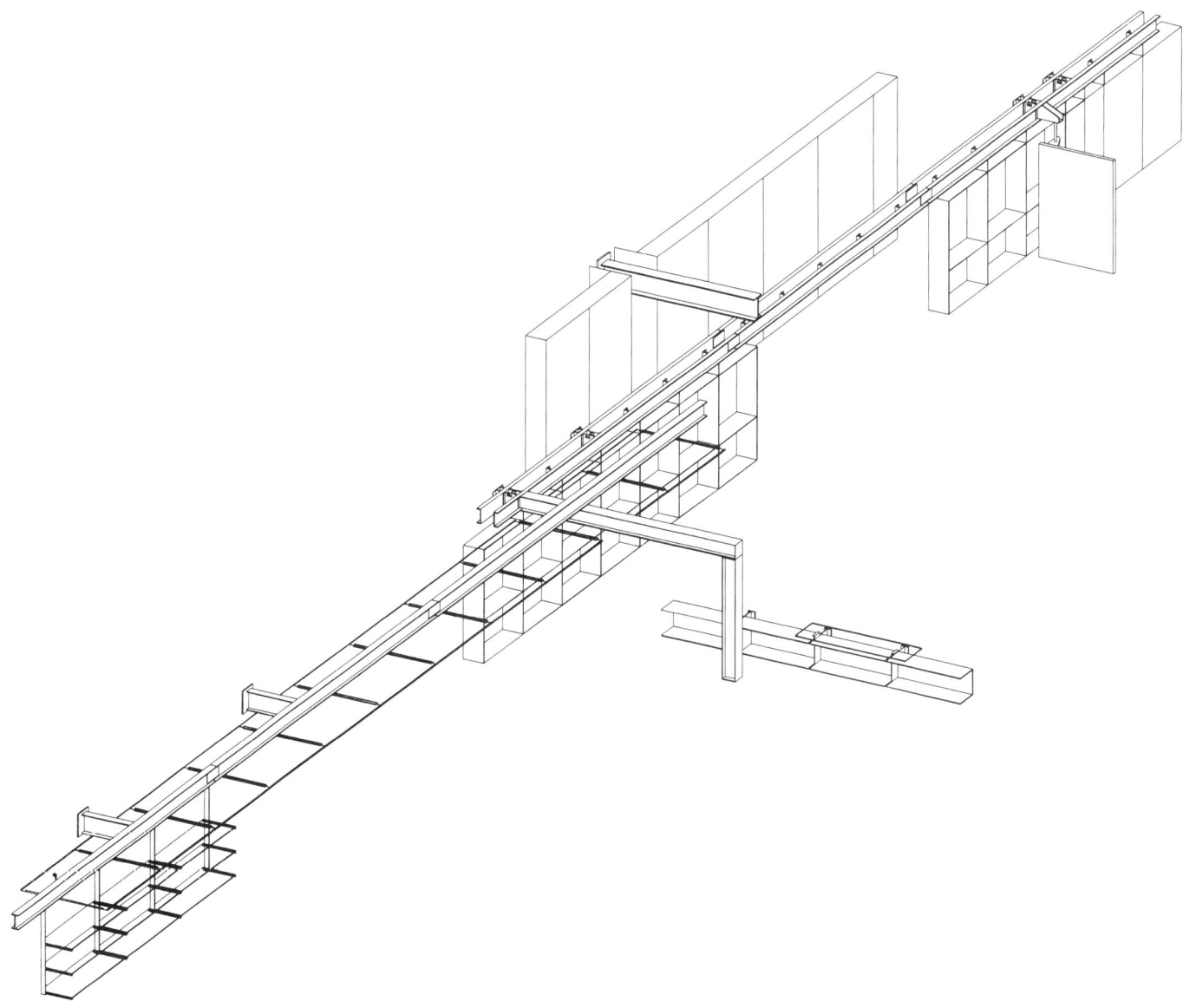

Axonometry of the suspended structure

The project and the use of a
suspended structure have been
developed in a remarkable way: all
the pieces were designed and
produced individually and then later
assembled inside the apartment.

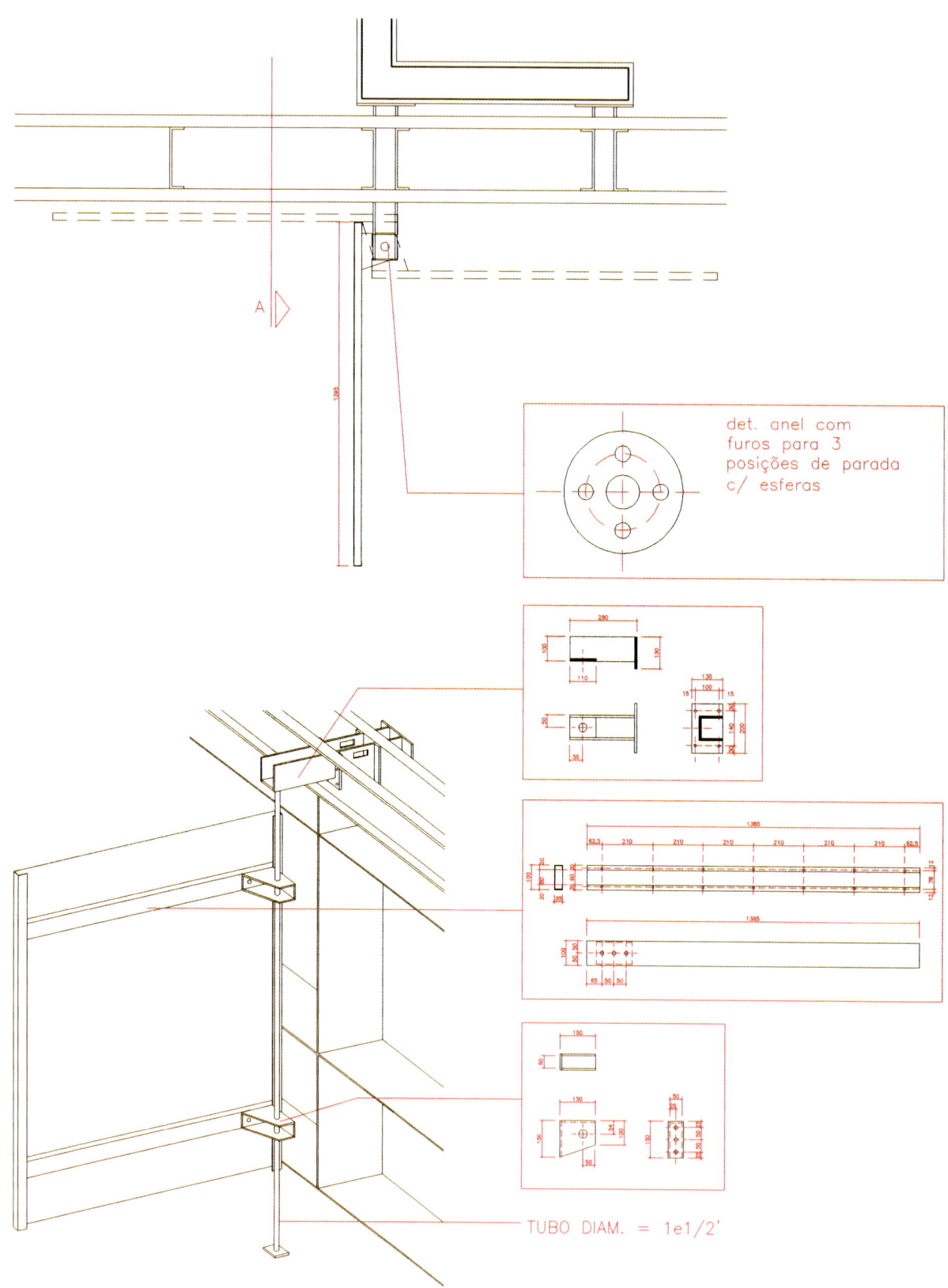

A

det. anel com
furos para 3
posições de parada
c/ esferas

TUBO DIAM. = 1e1/2'

Detail of the suspended structure

Urban Living Space in Berlin-Mitte

ABCARIUS + BURNS ARCHITECTURE DESIGN

This project was able to integrate and transform the traditional functions of a living space –sleeping, cooking, bathing, relaxing, etc.– by creating different and surprising spaces and utilizing a contemporary architectural language. This apartment, part a new building in the historic centre of Berlin, presents an urban habitat characterized by flexibility and functionality which constantly plays on the ambiguity between public and private space.

The floor consists of two parallel volumes which channel light towards the interior and whose doors and movable walls freely transform the space. Wheels have been placed on the bathtub; thus one can enjoy a refreshing bath on the balcony in summer or by the fire in winter. The water connections are integrated into practicable panels fitted flexible tubing. Other materials such as limestone or walnut have been used, as well as white lacquered surface areas to heighten luminosity.

Location: Berlin, Germany | **Contributors:** Nicole Fisher + Heike Buchfelder + York Arend | **Completion Date:** 2004 | **Area:** 100 m² | **Photography:** Ludger Paffrath

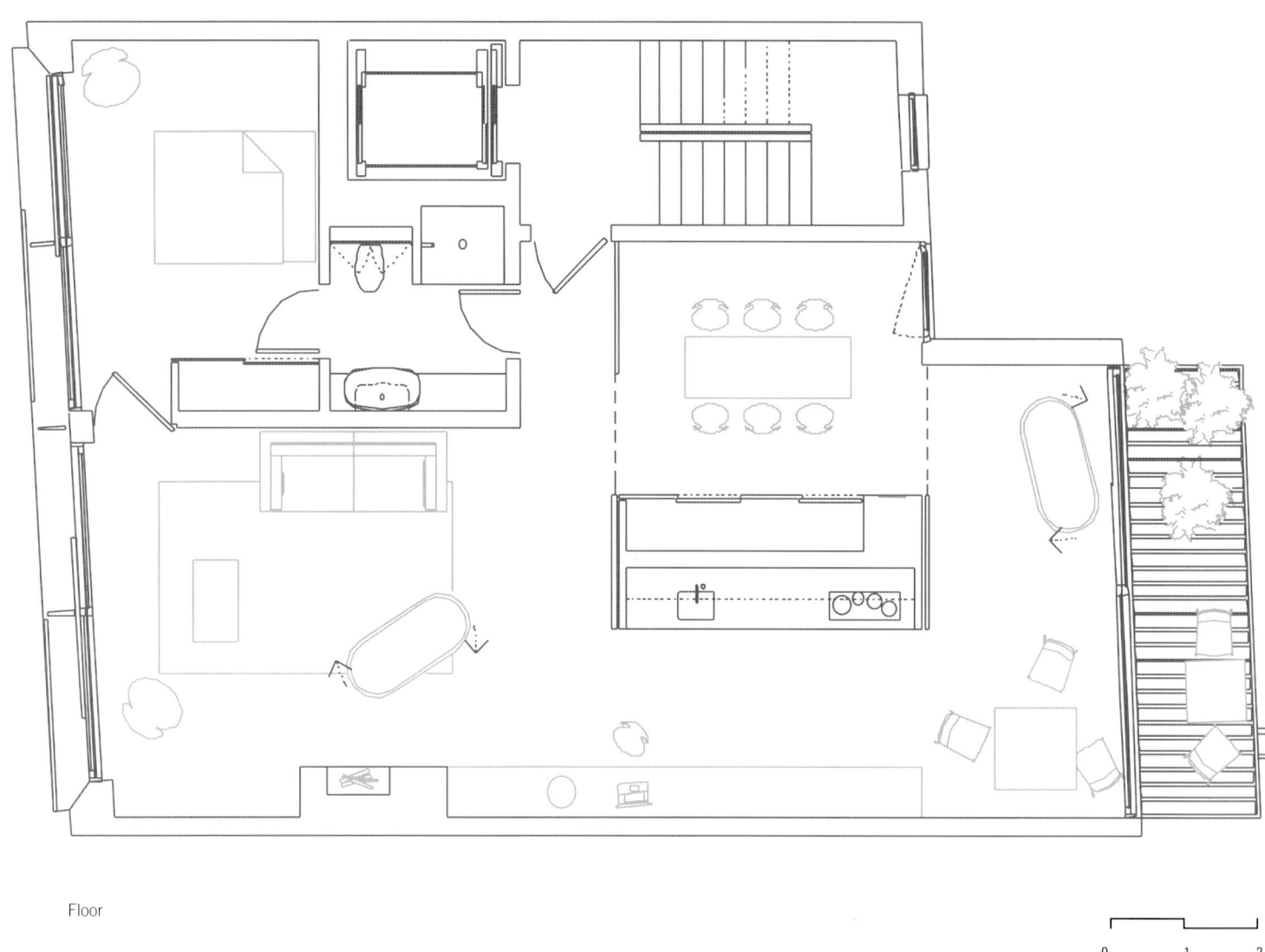

Floor

0   1   2

All the apartments enjoy ample
exterior spaces, either courtyards or
terraces, which reinforce the organic
character of these living spaces,
contrasting with the urban
environment of the building.

Urban Refuge

MORRIS SATO STUDIO

This New York apartment is a magnificent example of how to convert a small space of just 55 m² into a broad and personal refuge. The main axis of the operation is a curved wall which completely transforms the rectangular area of the original space creating both movement and freedom.

Due to the lack of fine views, the windows have been closed with screens that filter the light and lend continuity to the pure whiteness of the walls. Flooring with various colours and materials and designer furniture create an interior landscape of cool elegant tones. The main space is highlighted by an acrylic table with a metal rod base fitted with LED which reflects on the ceiling, bathing it in a metallic blue light. Undoubtedly this is one of the more interesting features of the project, along with the building's structure which has been partially exposed, as if it were urban architectural remains. The result is an abstract interior full of details establishing a constant dialogue between material aspects and colour.

Location: New York, New York, USA I **Completion Date:** 2004 I **Area:** 55 m² I **Photography:** Michael Moran

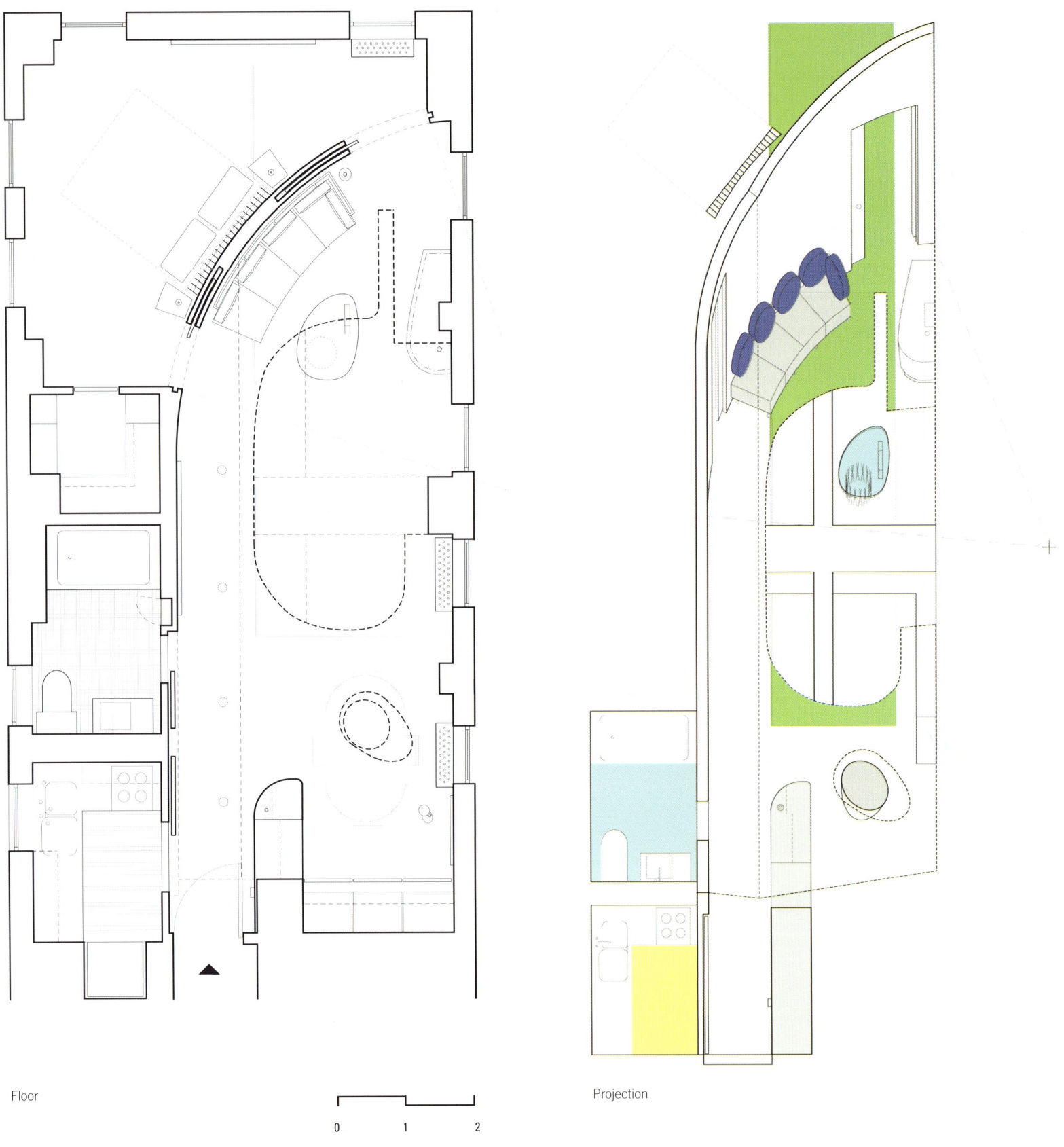

Floor

0   1   2

Projection

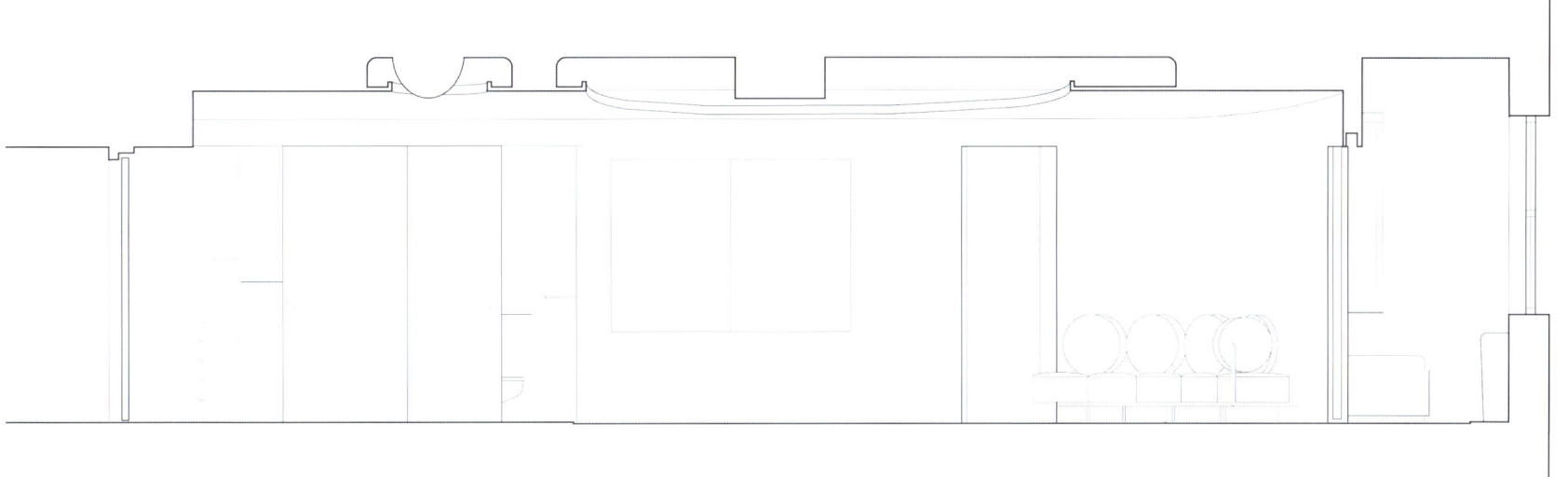

Longitudinal section

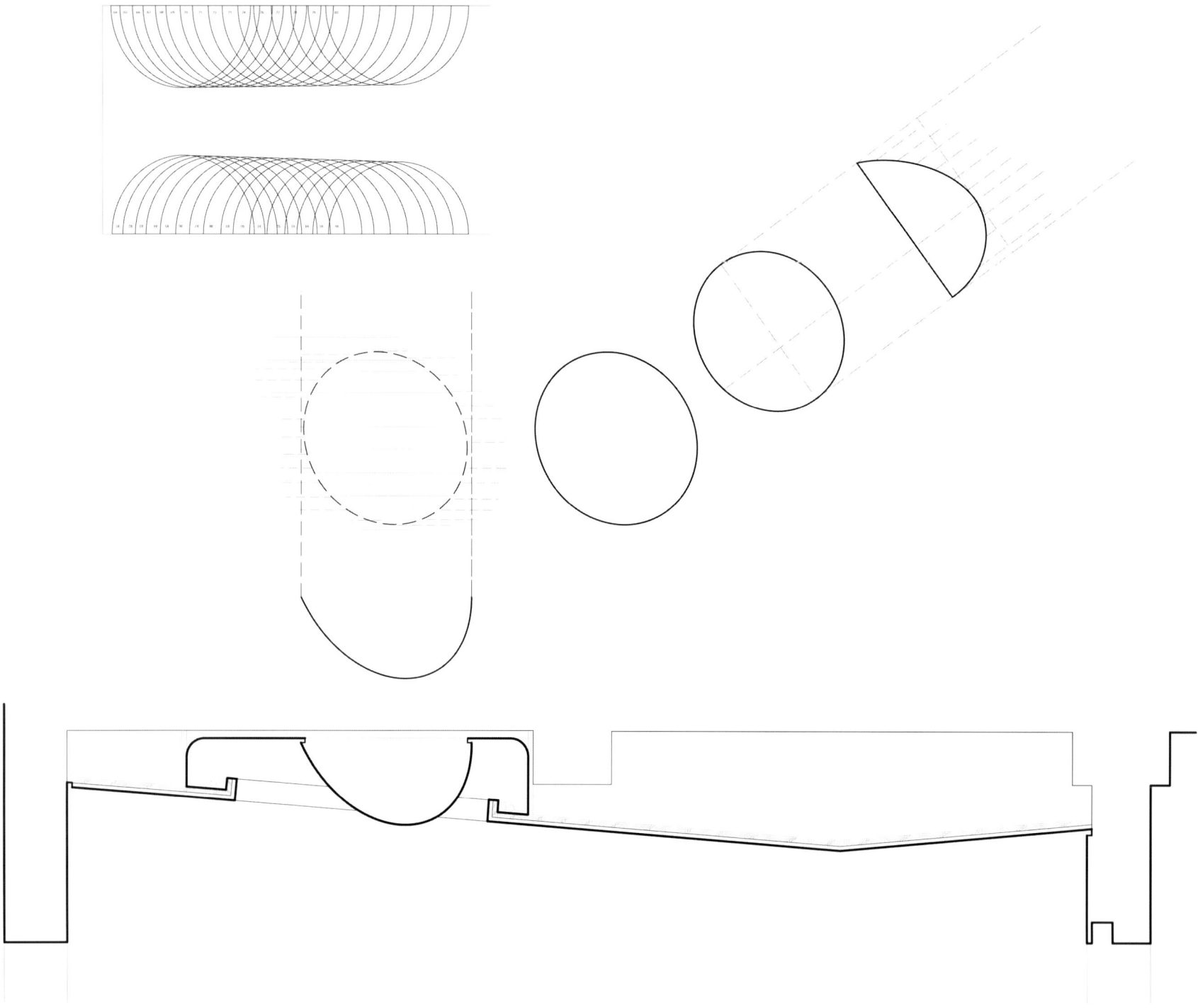

Ceiling detail

Hanging from the ceiling is a delicate
oval element –which the architects
call a "chandelier"– strikingly formed
by 160 plates of "foam" and an
identical number of layers of liquid
plaster.

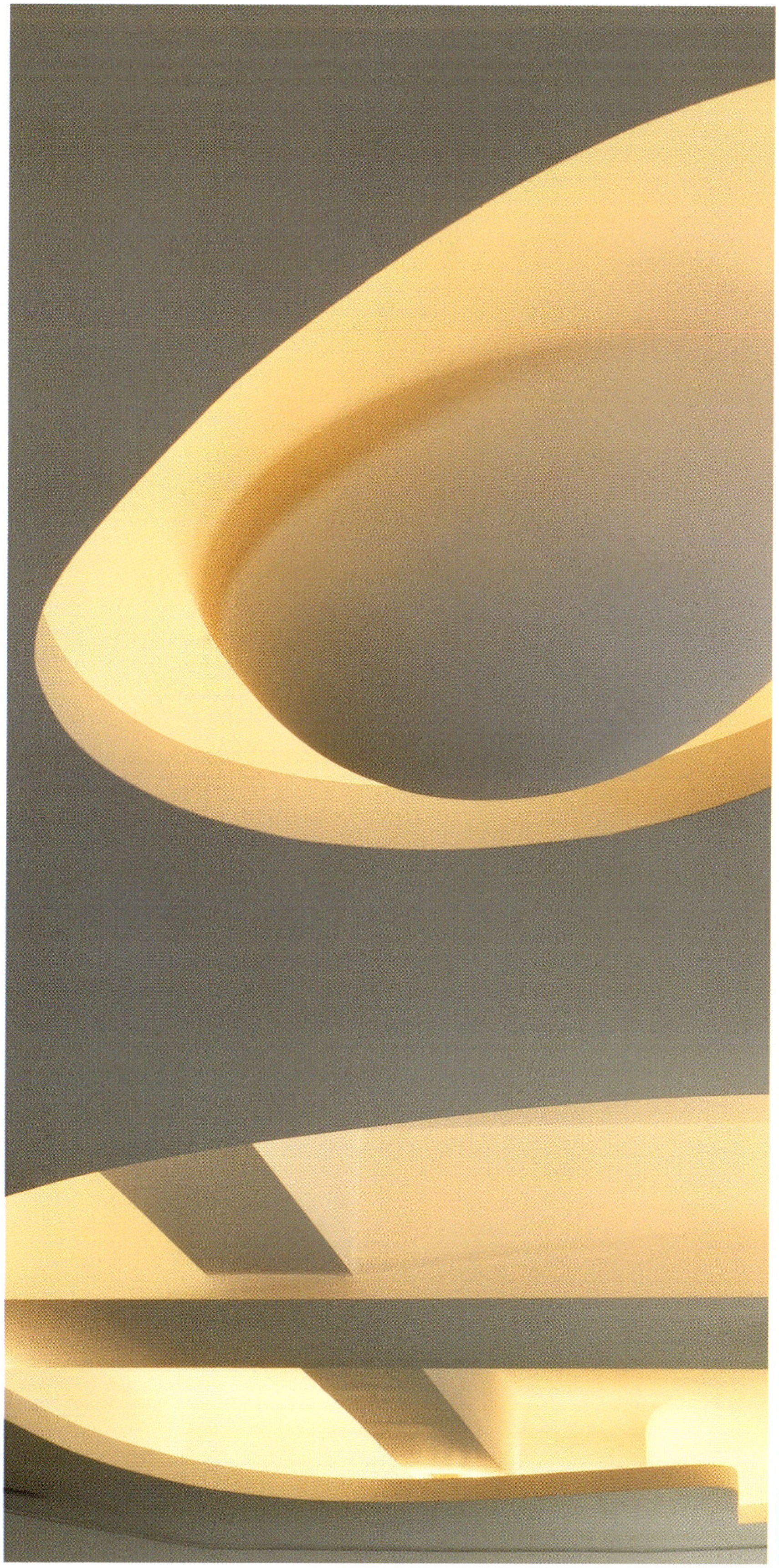

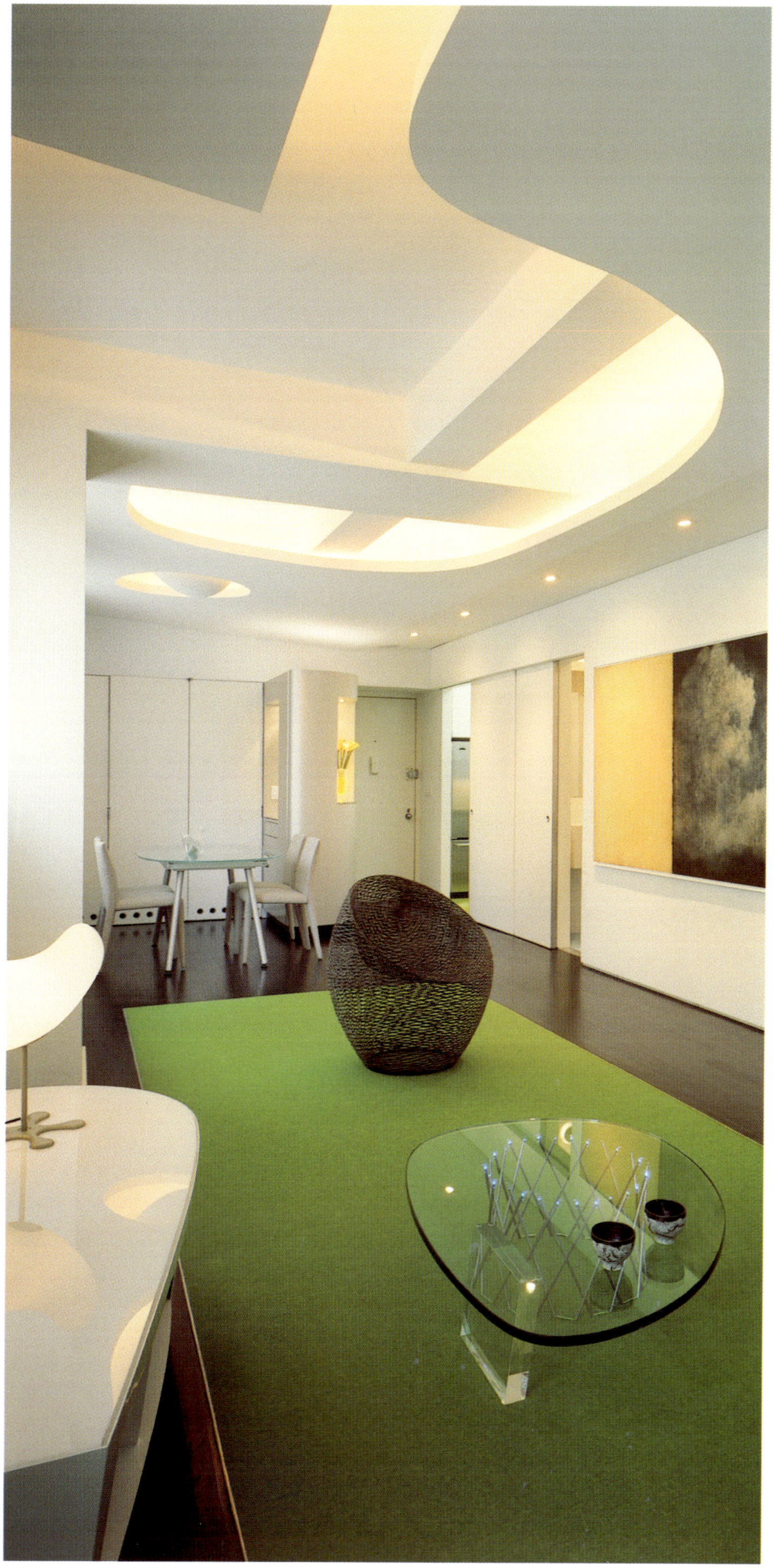

Renovated Penthouse in Andorra

ELISABET FAURA + GERARD VECIANA/ARTEKS

One of the principal objectives of this project was to achieve maximum clarity, as the apartment had several perimeter walls, either dummy ones or ones only open to the interior courtyards. To obtain a fluid space while keeping in mind the needs of the client –a single person who occasionally receives many guests– each wall was examined individually in order to attain the correct thickness, texture, and colour. They have been set in such a way which allows natural light to flow throughout the living space. A dynamic dialogue was thus established between the materials of the apartment: flooring of white resin concrete, walnut parquet, and walls made from slate, Wengue, or painted in green, red or black. In terms of distribution, the living room was discarded, with the idea of converting the entire penthouse into a large living area, where the kitchen-dining area was the main space facing a large window wall. To accommodate guests, a room has been set in the space above, as a refuge, quite in step with owner's interest in the alpine style.

Location: Andorra la Vella, Andorra I **Completion Date:** 2003 I **Area:** 117 m² I **Photography:** Eugeni Pons

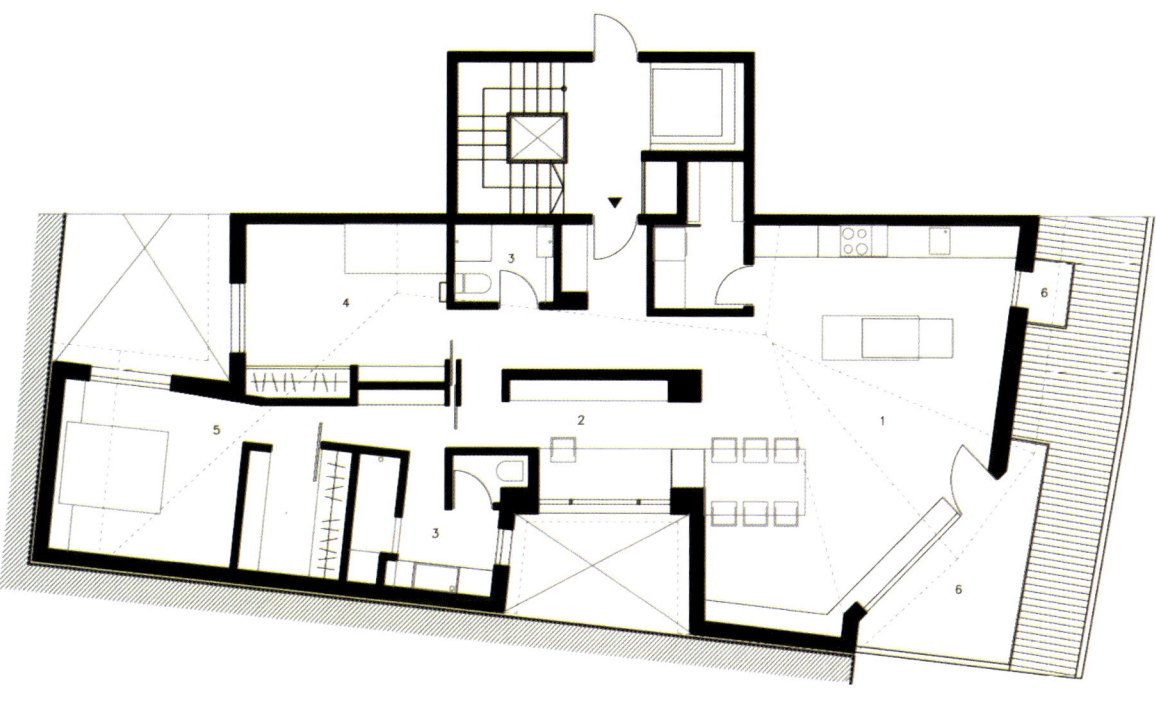

Floor

0 1 2

Cross section

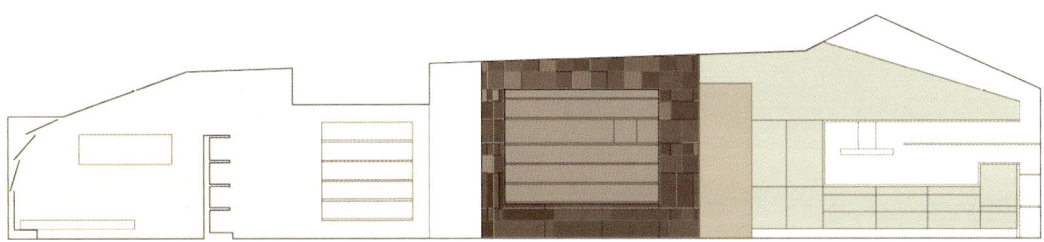

Longitudinal section

The entrance wall outlines the
circulation and brings together the
reading and work areas of the library
and the rear area.

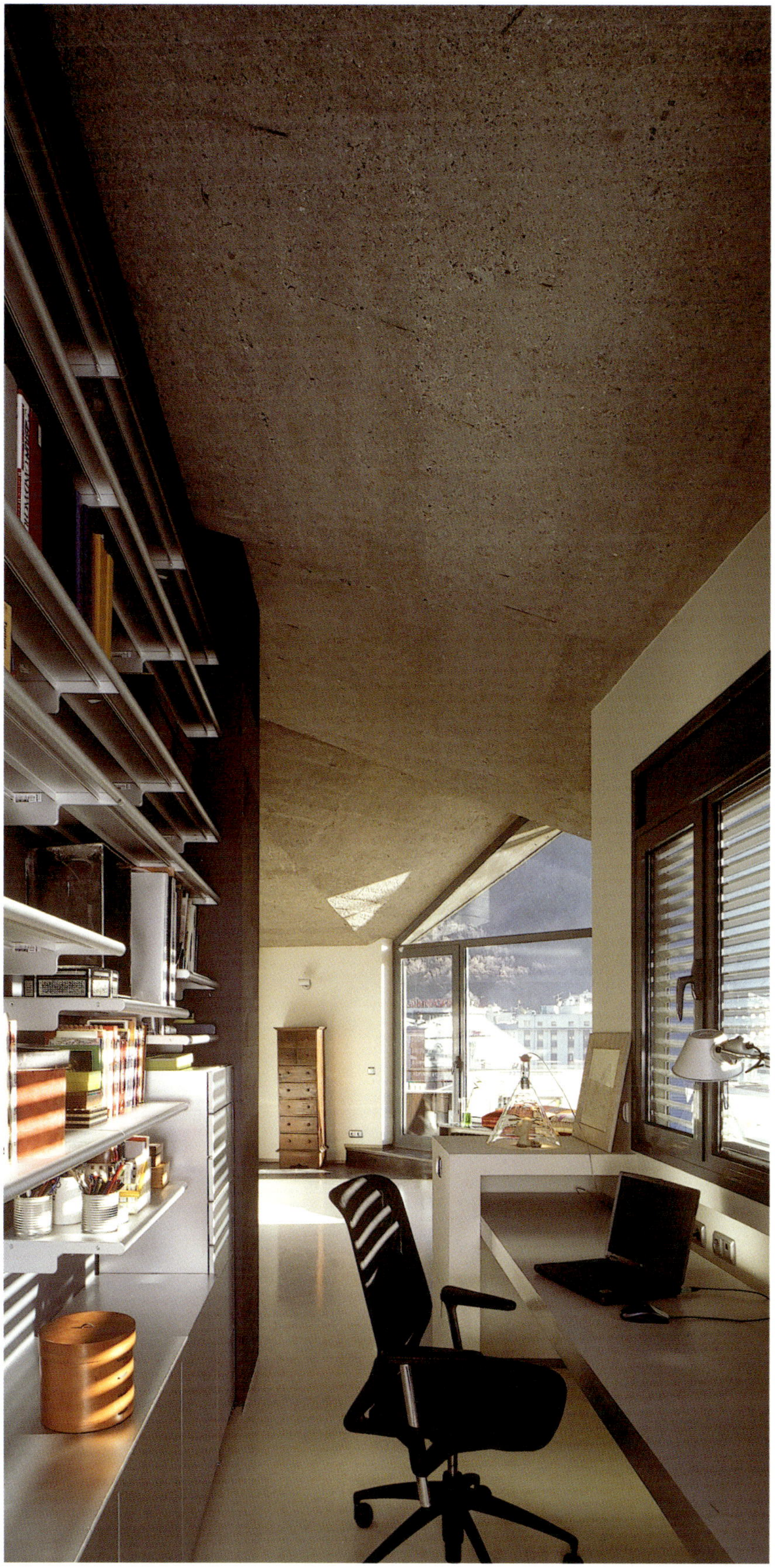
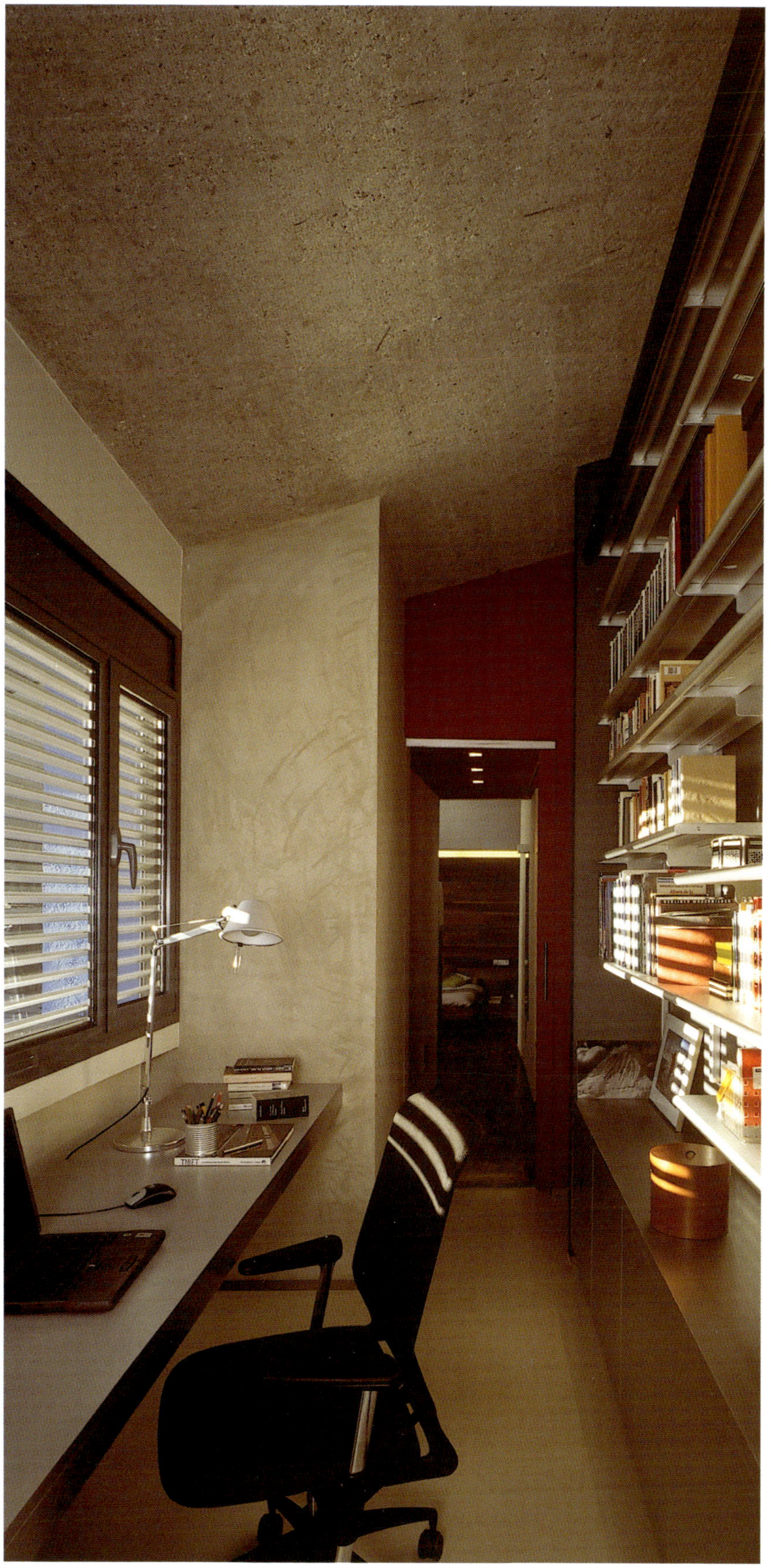

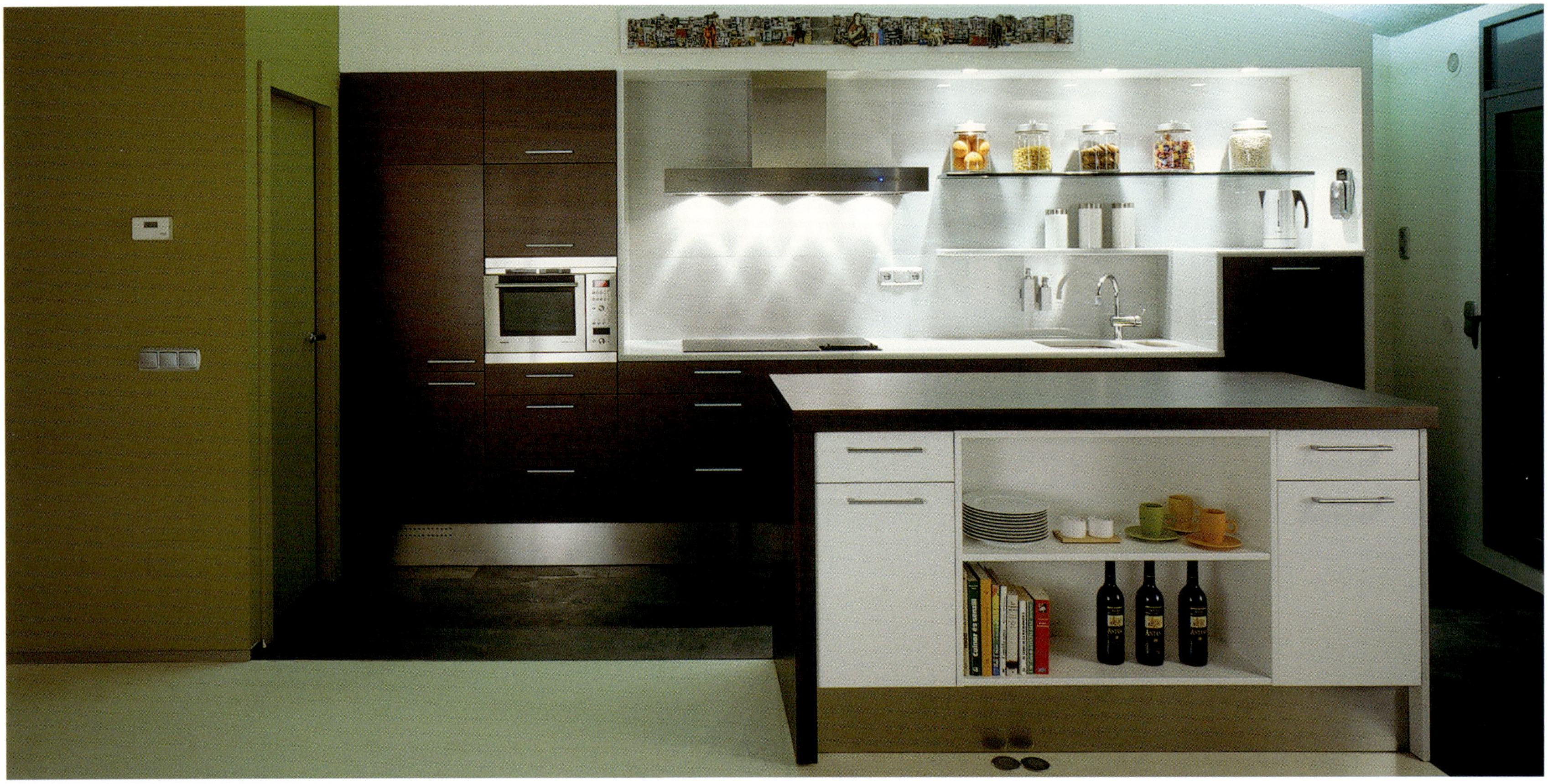

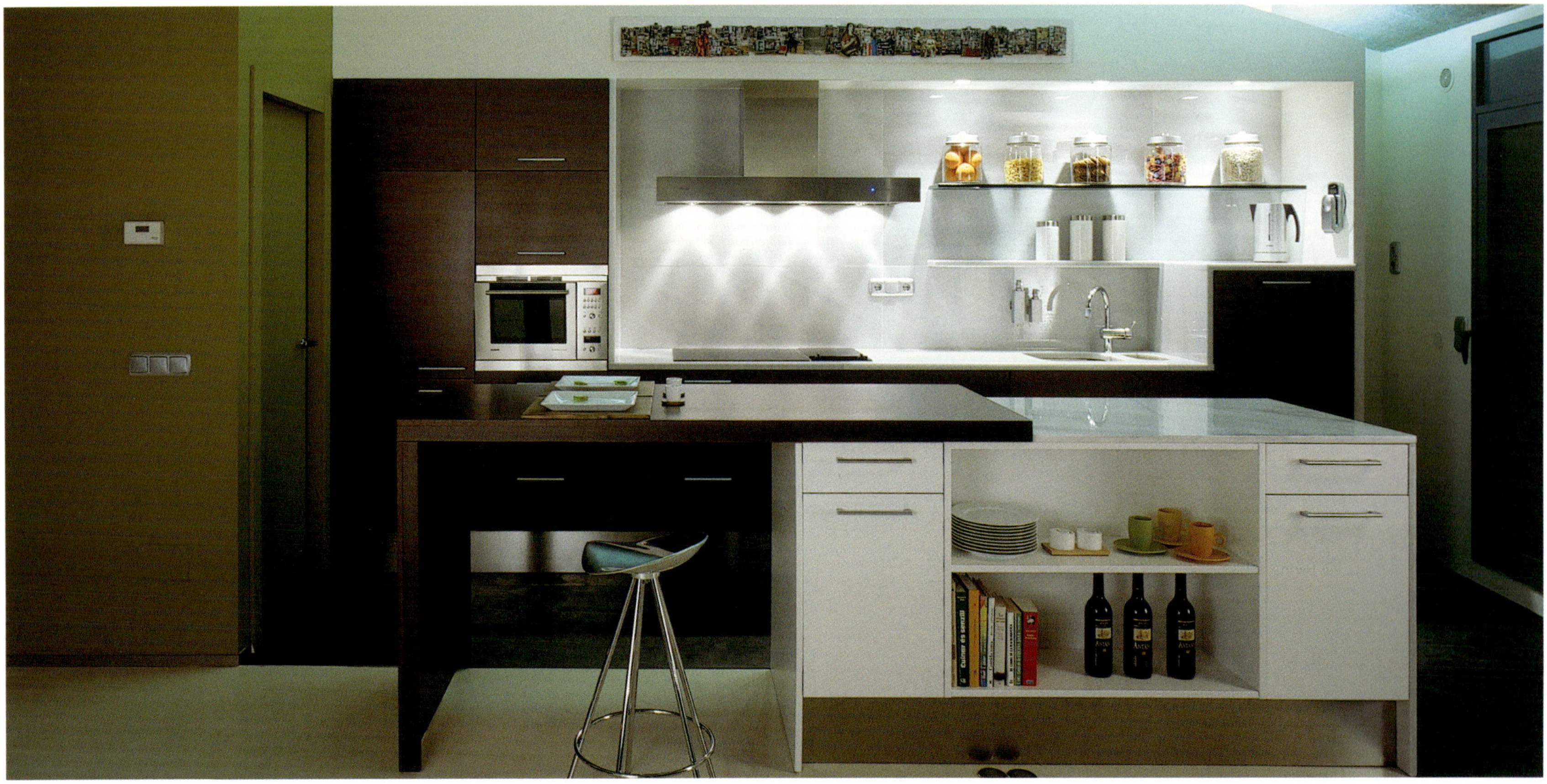

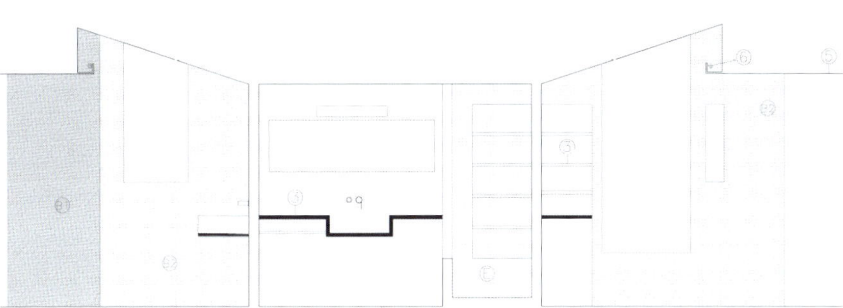

Bathroom elevation

Family Loft

GIOVANNI GUIOTTO/INDESIGN ARCHITETTURA E DISEGNO INDUSTRIALE

This project had to unite the characteristics of a space with industrial origins with the needs of a five-member family, thus leading the way to its apparently contradictory name. By using a precise distribution of space within the ambiguity typical of a loft, both privacy and flexibility were able to be provided at the same time.

The entire space enjoys a generous volume with five-meter high ceilings where white predominates –from the solid fir parquet to the vaulted ceiling–. A mezzanine containing the sleeping area occupies nearly half the floor space and lets the main area have higher ceilings, with the bedroom opening out on to this space.

Two large lacquered volumes that demarcate the kitchen and serve as an entry point have been inserted below the mezzanine as if they were moving containers, emphasizing the temporary nature of their respective spaces. One of the volumes is the guest bedroom, completely glassed in facing the living room; the other is a service area which transforms into a photo lab.

Location: Venice, Italy I **Contributors:** Giancarlo Giuriati + Sergio Nardin I **Completion Date:** 2003 I **Area:** 245 m² I **Photography:** Matteo Piazza

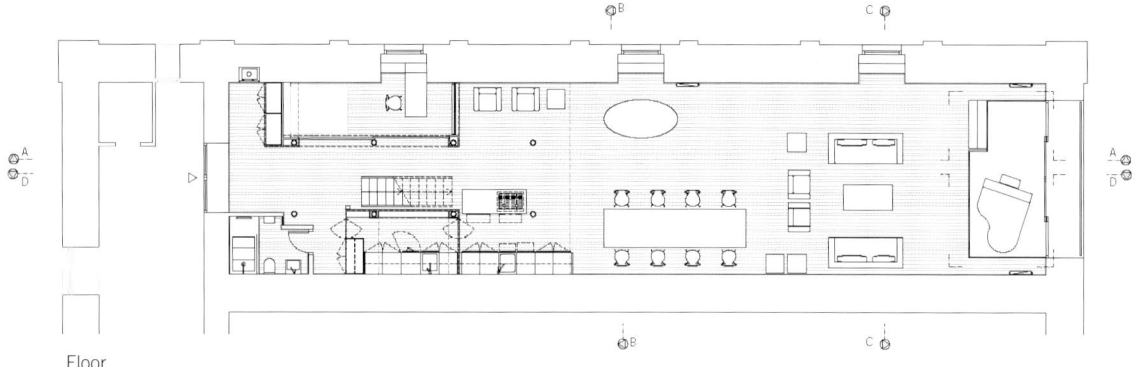

Floor

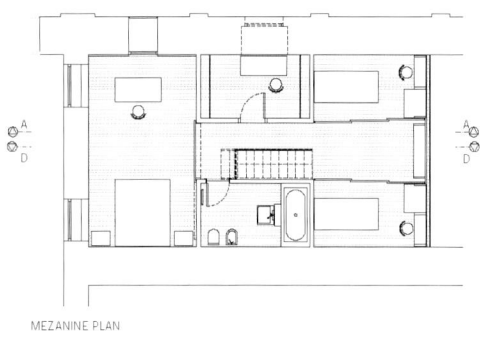

MEZZANINE PLAN

Mezzanine

0   1   2

The entire length of the space can be
seen from the entrance of the living space, as well as the staircase to the mezzanine and counterpoint of colour between
the furniture and the white interior.

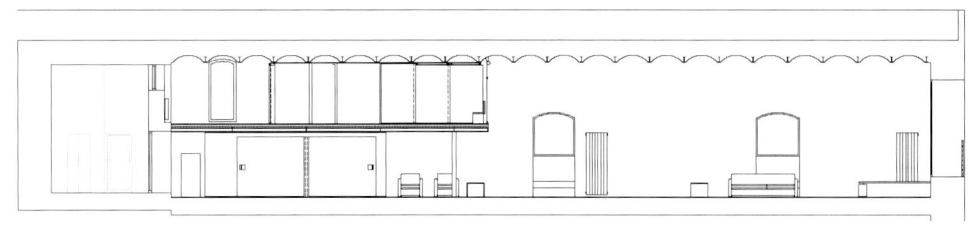

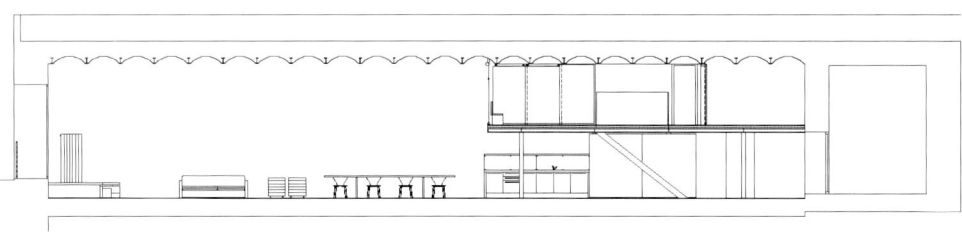

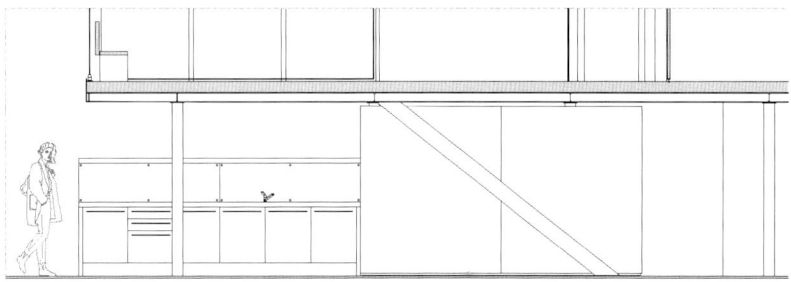

Longitudinal sections

The main bedroom is the only truly traditional bedroom, as it closes off with a large sliding ceiling-to-floor door.

Jordi/Aida Living Space

JOSEP LLOBET

Ever since its construction back in the twenties, this centrally-located apartment in Girona has suffered numerous and unfortunate transformations which have brought it to a most deplorable state. The first rehabilitating step consisted in tearing down the interior walls, leaving only the structural ones in order to attain more ample bedrooms in accordance with a more contemporary lifestyle. The new interior draws a fluid line without obstacles, but at the same time clearly differentiates the spaces. The kitchen, lined with moving glass panels, has been set next to the entrance in the central nucleus of the living space and its main focal point is a large island, which was designed by the architect; it can be used both for cooking as well as for receiving or entertaining guests.

The kitchen, dining room, bathrooms and bedrooms have been placed over teak flooring to set them apart from the large living area, which conserves its original mosaic tile flooring. The result is an atemporal apartment with a careful design and a simple and serene ambience.

Location: Girona, Spain | **Contributors:** Nuria Feijoo + Natalia Ojeda + Alice Ruggeri + Anna Vela | **Completion Date:** 2003 | **Area:** 160 m² | **Photography:** Eugeni Pons

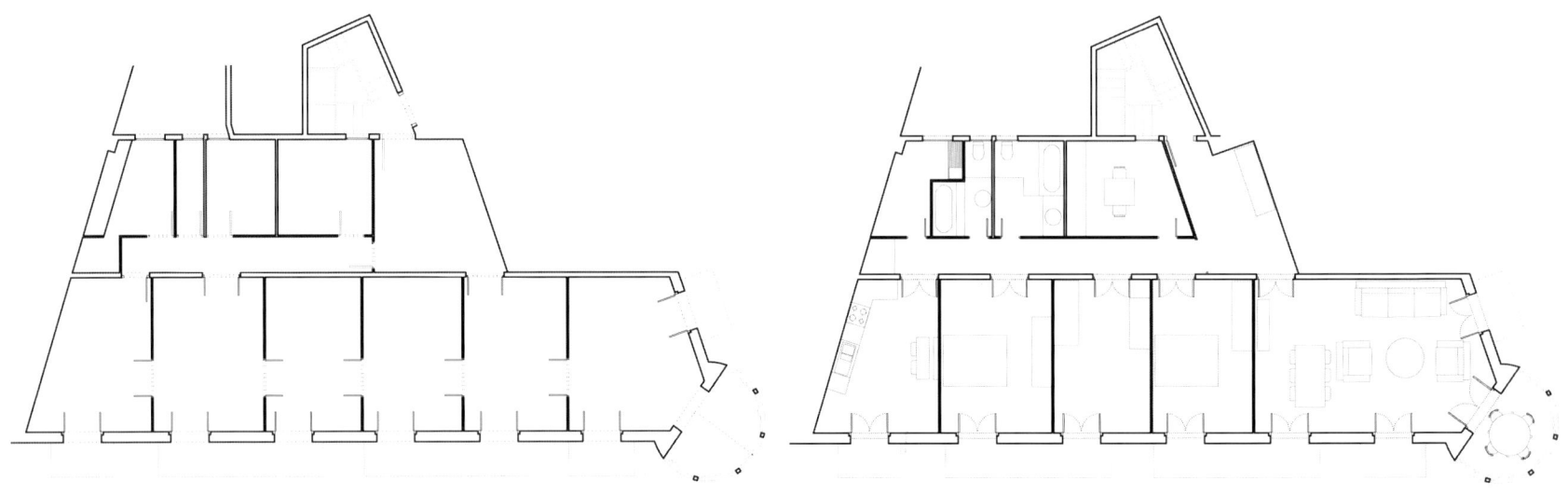

Floor plan from 1928

Floor plan from 1995

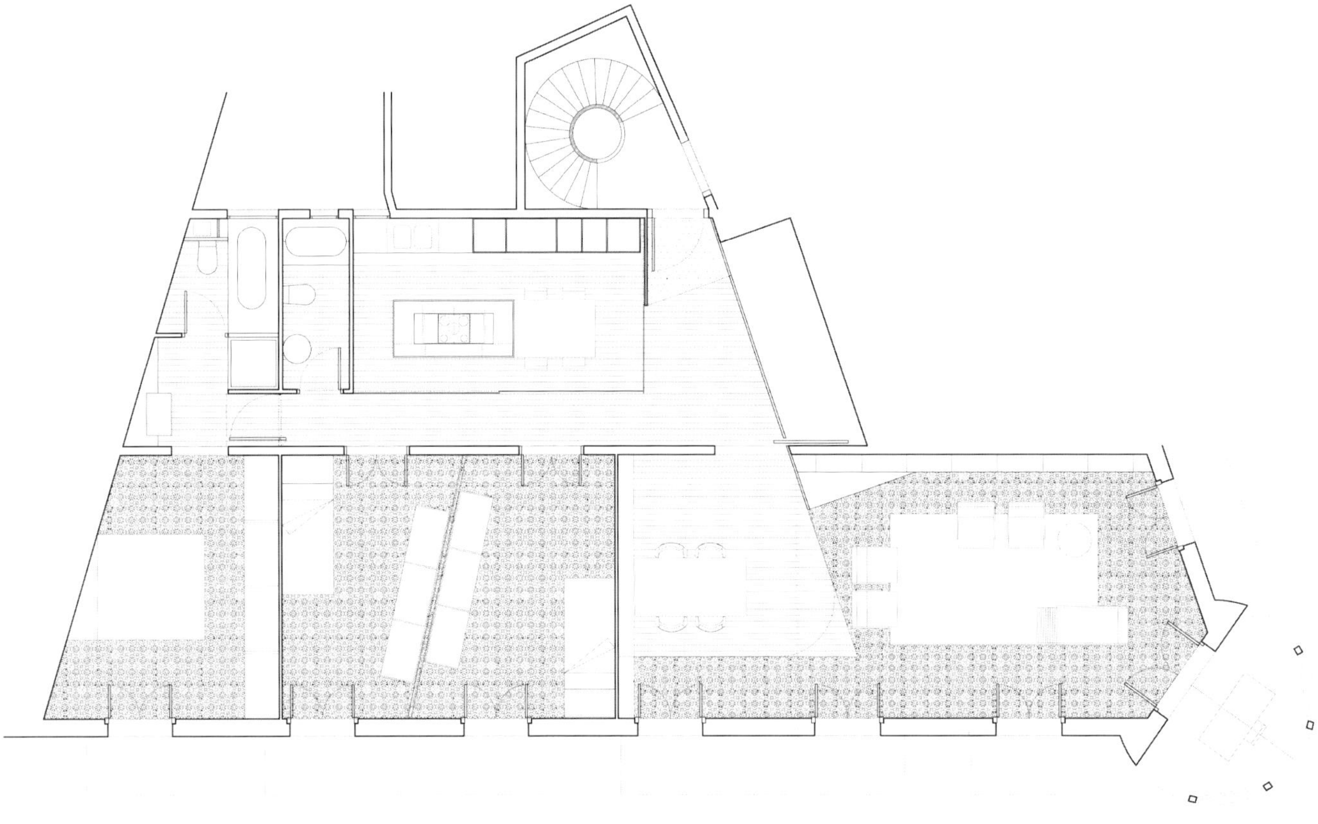

Current floor plan

0   1   2

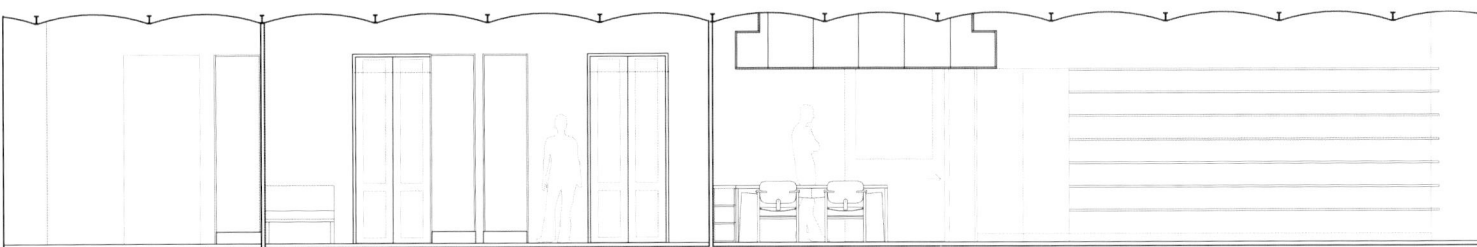

Longitudinal section

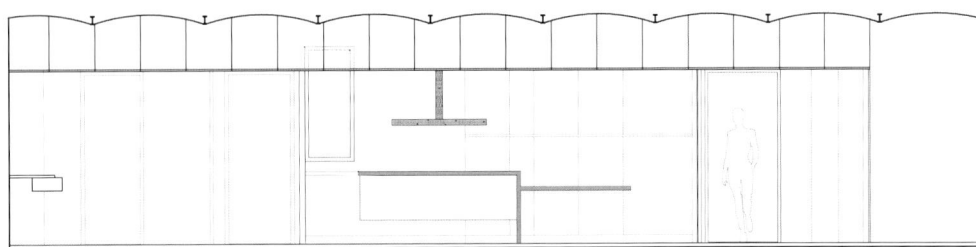

Longitudinal section of the kitchen

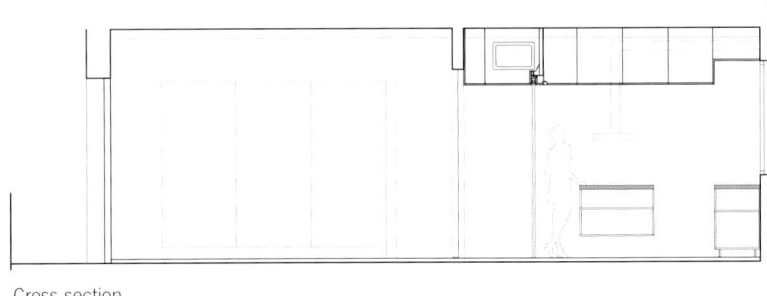

Cross section

The furniture was designed by the
architect, and includes the kitchen,
dining room, shelves and cabinets
that stand out for their linear sim-
plicity and eminent practical sense.

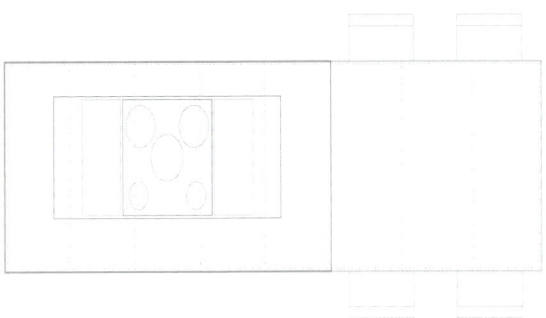

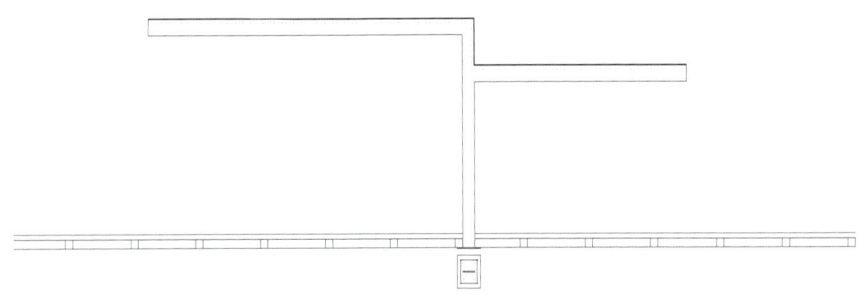

Kitchen detail

Slender

DEADLINE/WWW.DEADLINE.DE

Slender is a singular project: a single family house built in Berlin's historical centre on top of a narrow building dating from the period between the wars. The challenge was to extract all the architectural potential of a reduced area of just 19 x 5 m and create ample spaces with simple lines and wide openings. The house presents a personal idea of what living space represents, where space flows and each area is determined by its use. Apart from this functional aspect, the daily routine is organized in a constant circular motion from the private areas to the common ones, with a suspended sleeping area as the starting and finishing point for such a pattern.

The finishes, in exposed or painted concrete, are simple and draw out the spatial qualities and construction elements. Likewise, a large curved window wall spanning two floors stands out and provides abundant natural light to the common areas. On the roof, a large hanging garden reminds us we are in a house and provides a magnificent view of the city.

Location: Berlin, Germany | **Completion Date:** 2002 | **Area:** 130 m² | **Photography:** Ludger Paffrath

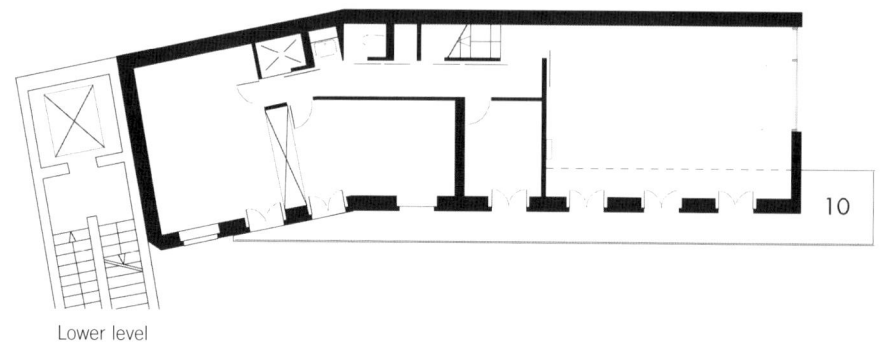

Lower level

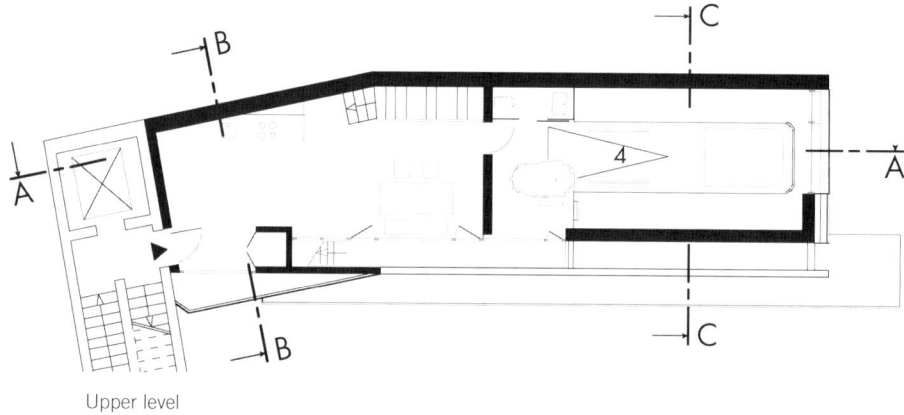

Upper level

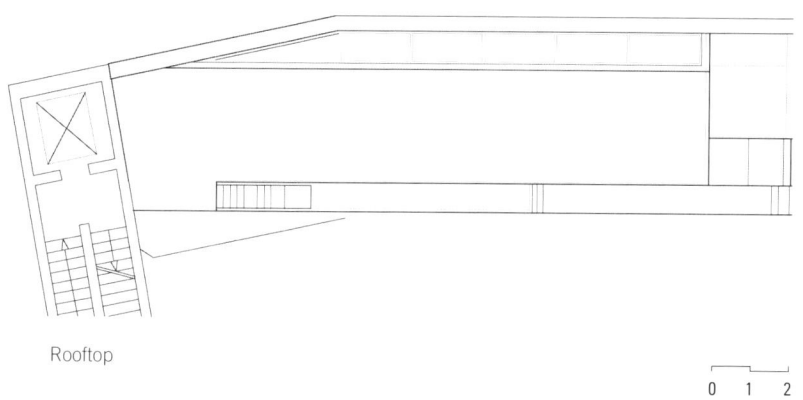

Rooftop

0 1 2

The large curved window wall is extended into part of the ceiling; the sleeping area, a suspended platform located above the main space, is thus stands open to the sky.

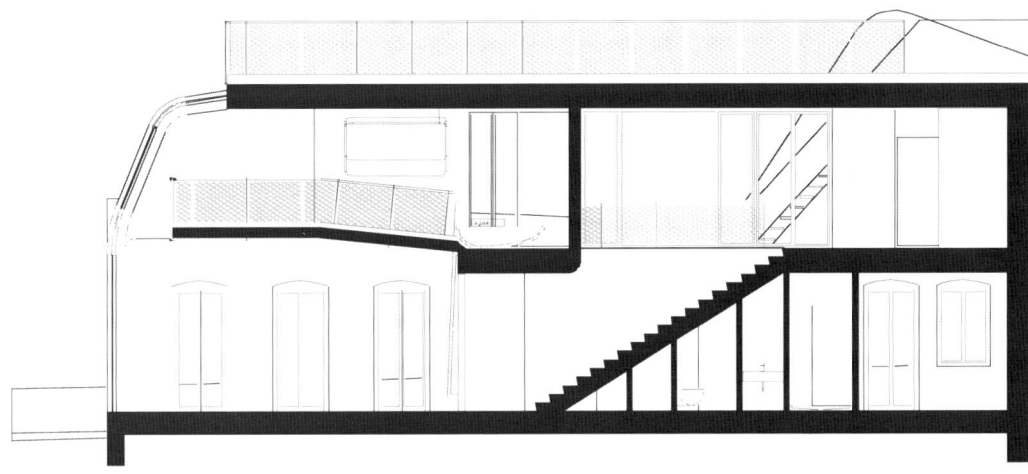

Longitudinal section

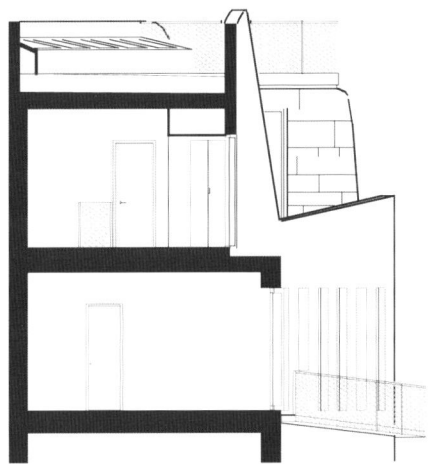
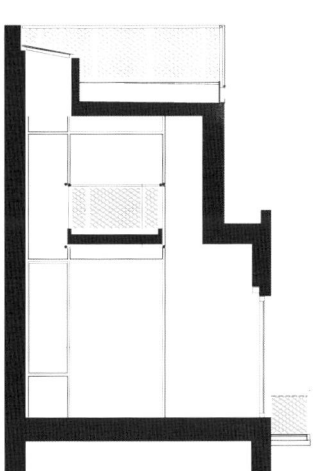

Cross sections

Pasaje Sert Loft

HÉCTOR RESTREPO CALVO / HERES ARQUITECTURA

Located in a former textile factory from the 19th century that has been completely rehabilitated, this living space is a fine example of a residential renovation in an industrial setting. The principal objective was to obtain a diaphanous space which would also guarantee privacy, which is to say, a loft that lends a certain intimacy to its occupants without renouncing spatial continuity.

The operation focused on placing the central volume between the original cast pillars, as if it was a cube containing all the service areas of the living space –kitchen, bathroom, toilet– and separating the interior into two distinct parts. The flooring helps this separation; one side, the common area and living area, has water-resistant sandstone and the other, the bedroom, is defined by a galvanized steel plate floor. The kitchen, strategically located on one side of the central volume, adds colour to the cube with its red siltstone work surface and also constitutes an ambiguous filter that allows for a dialogue between the two areas of the house.

Location: Barcelona, Spain I **Completion Date:** 2003 I **Area:** 145 m² I **Photography:** Jordi Miralles

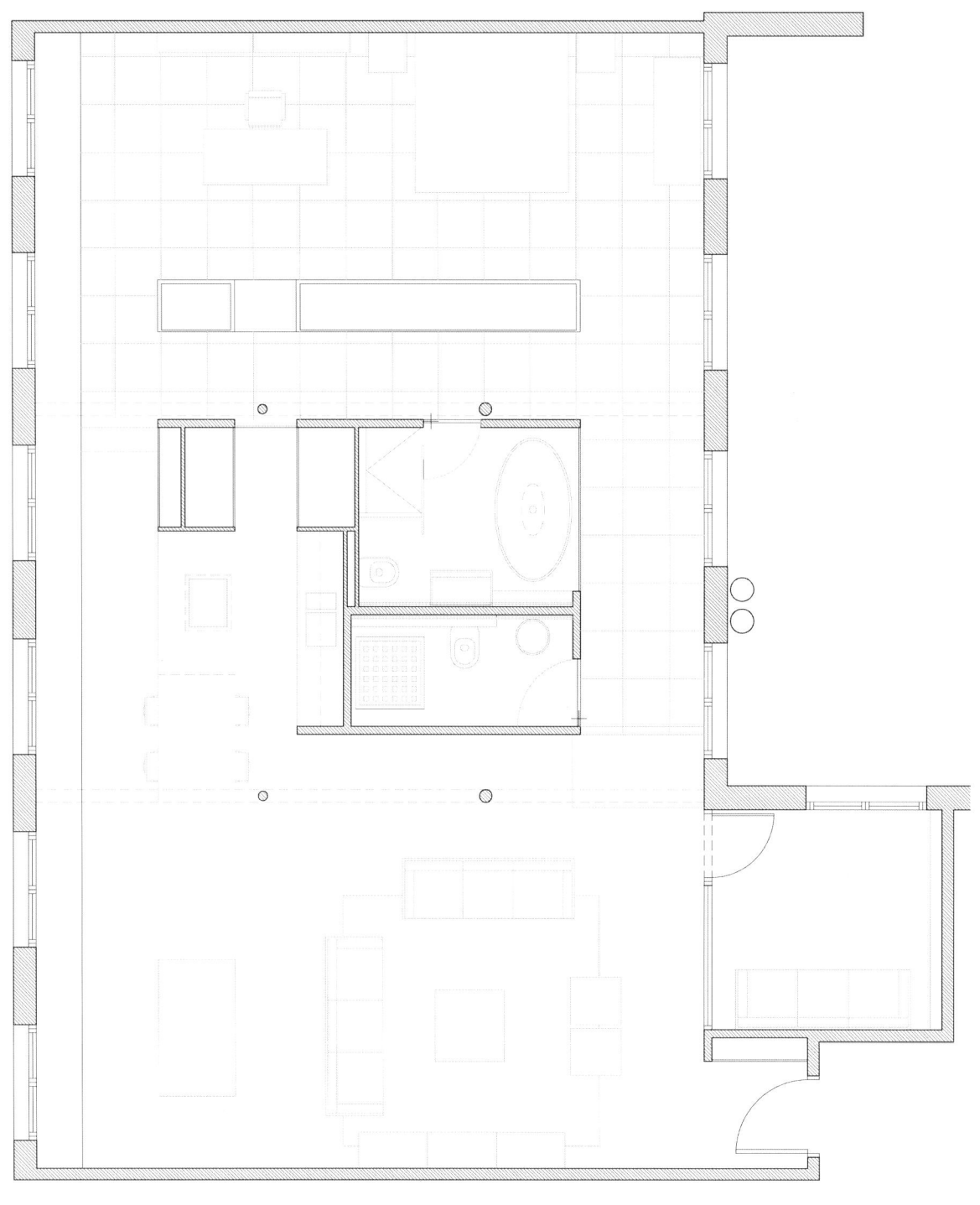

Floor

0   1   2

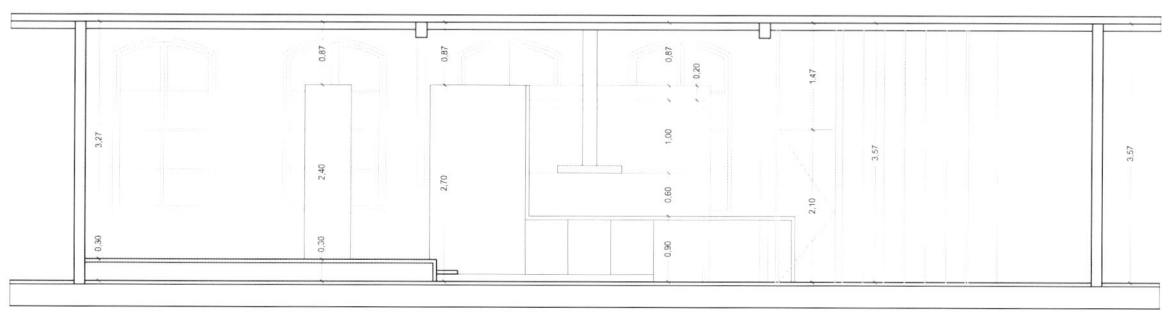

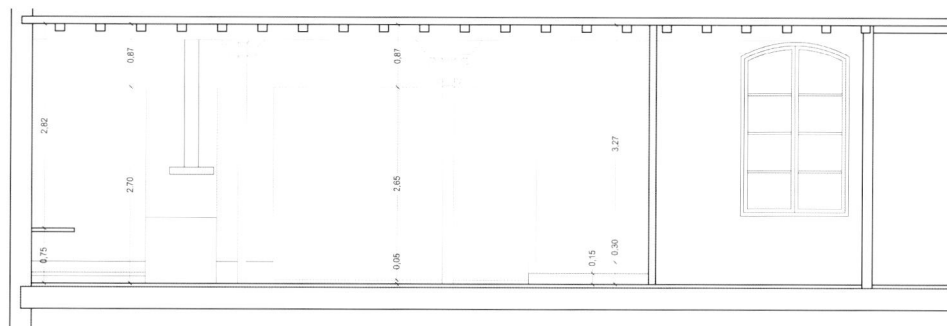

Longitudinal sections

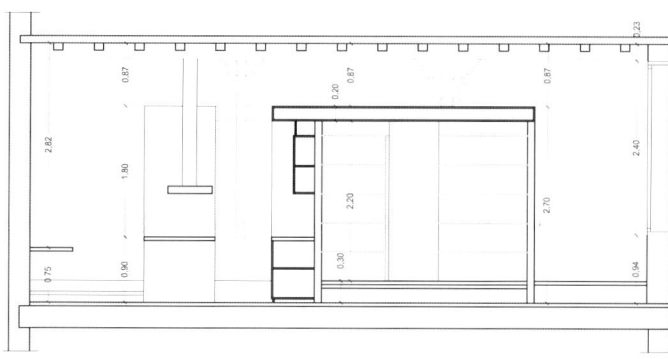

Cross section

Kaufman Loft

STEFANIA RINALDI/STUDIO RINALDI

In comparison to the current trend toward diaphanous spaces, this apartment is a fine example of the contrary, as it has been divided for specific reasons. The design of this loft accentuates its original characteristics, such as ample lighting and spaciousness, but at the same time it adapts to the needs of a small family. To do this, the ceiling height was raised and the necessary divisions were installed but fluidity and the continuity of the spaces was still maintained by using translucent doors.

The common areas find their highlight in the kitchen, a space integrated in the large dining-living room which is intended as a leisure area. Special attention has been paid to details and finishes as the use of different paint colours and flooring materials, such as marble, terrazzo, and walnut parquet to distinguish the spaces. The result is a family apartment with characteristic New York sophistication.

Location: New York, NY, USA | **Completion Date:** 2004 | **Area:** 185 m² | **Photography:** Wade Zimmerman

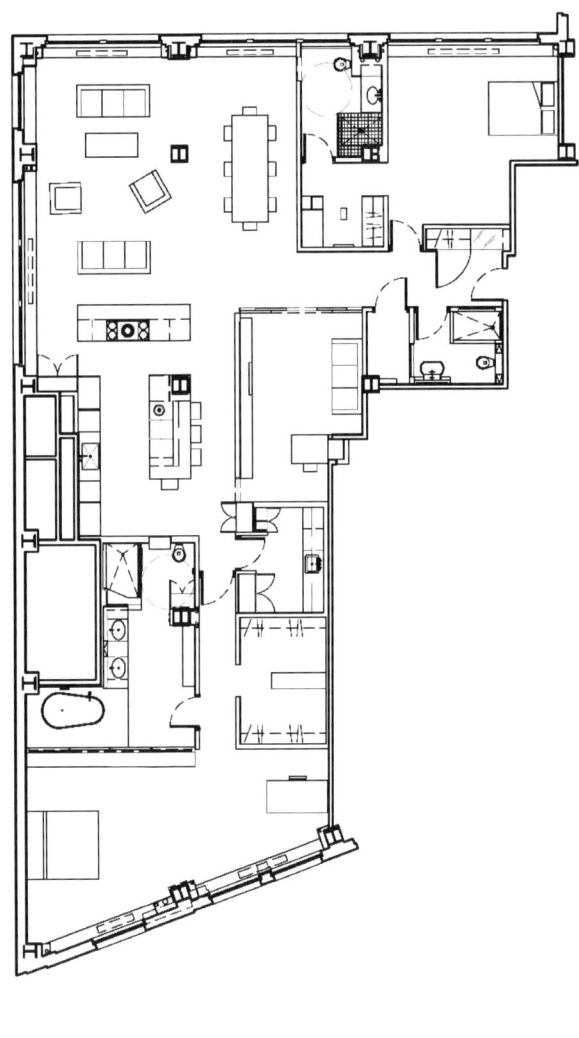

Floor

0   2   4

The integration of the kitchen with the
living room transforms the main area
into a dynamic and informal space
without losing the sophisticated air of
the entire apartment.

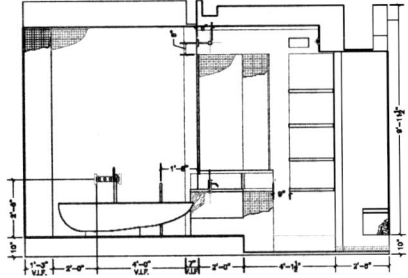 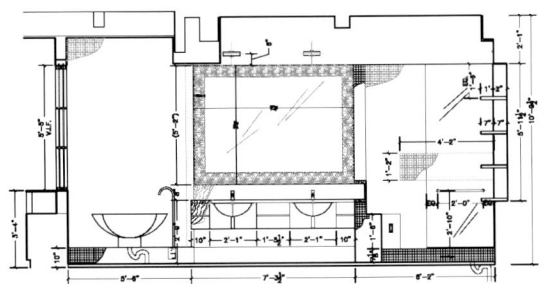

Bathroom elevations

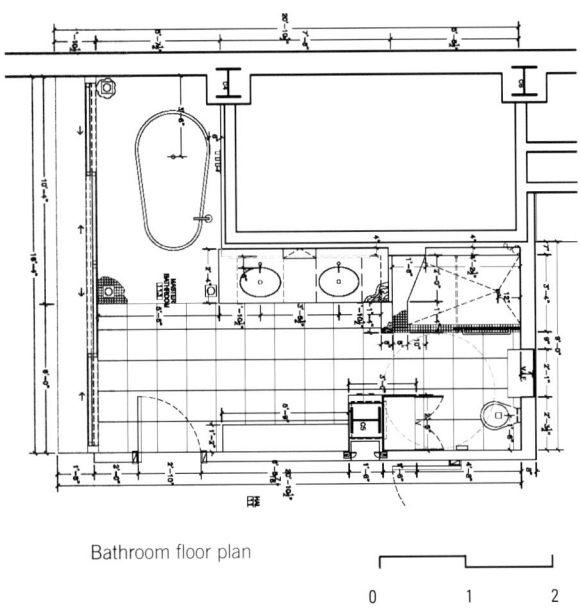

Bathroom floor plan

0   1   2

The most prominent features in the
main bathroom are the sliding
windows opening on to the adjacent
bedroom and the variety of materials:
marble facing, mosaic flooring and
walnut-panelled furniture.

Steve House

MARCO GUIDO SAVORELLI ARCHITETTO

The objective of this complete renovation project was to unite all its functions into a single habitable yet fragmented space. To do this, the interior walls were torn down and the structure was emphasized in order to become a skeleton for articulating the three main areas of the living space. The doors were replaced by movable ceiling-to-floor panels which, once closed, perfectly integrate into the walls.
The lacquered rosewood furniture is specifically designed and forms a fundamental part of the project, thanks to its precise and elegant geometric lines. The central space holds the dining-living area and the kitchen –subtly hidden behind a half wall not reaching the ceiling– while the bedroom is highlighted by the bathtub and the bed's headboard, both in marble. The third space is an adaptable room for both working and relaxing, with a practicable stool and desk integrated into the wall furnishings.
Following the "feng shui" philosophy, the true goal of this project was to create a balanced and harmonious living space in the style of pure and contemporary lines.

Location: Milan, Italy | **Contributors:** Daniela Bernabei | **Completion Date:** 2003 | **Area:** 90 m² | **Photography:** Matteo Piazza

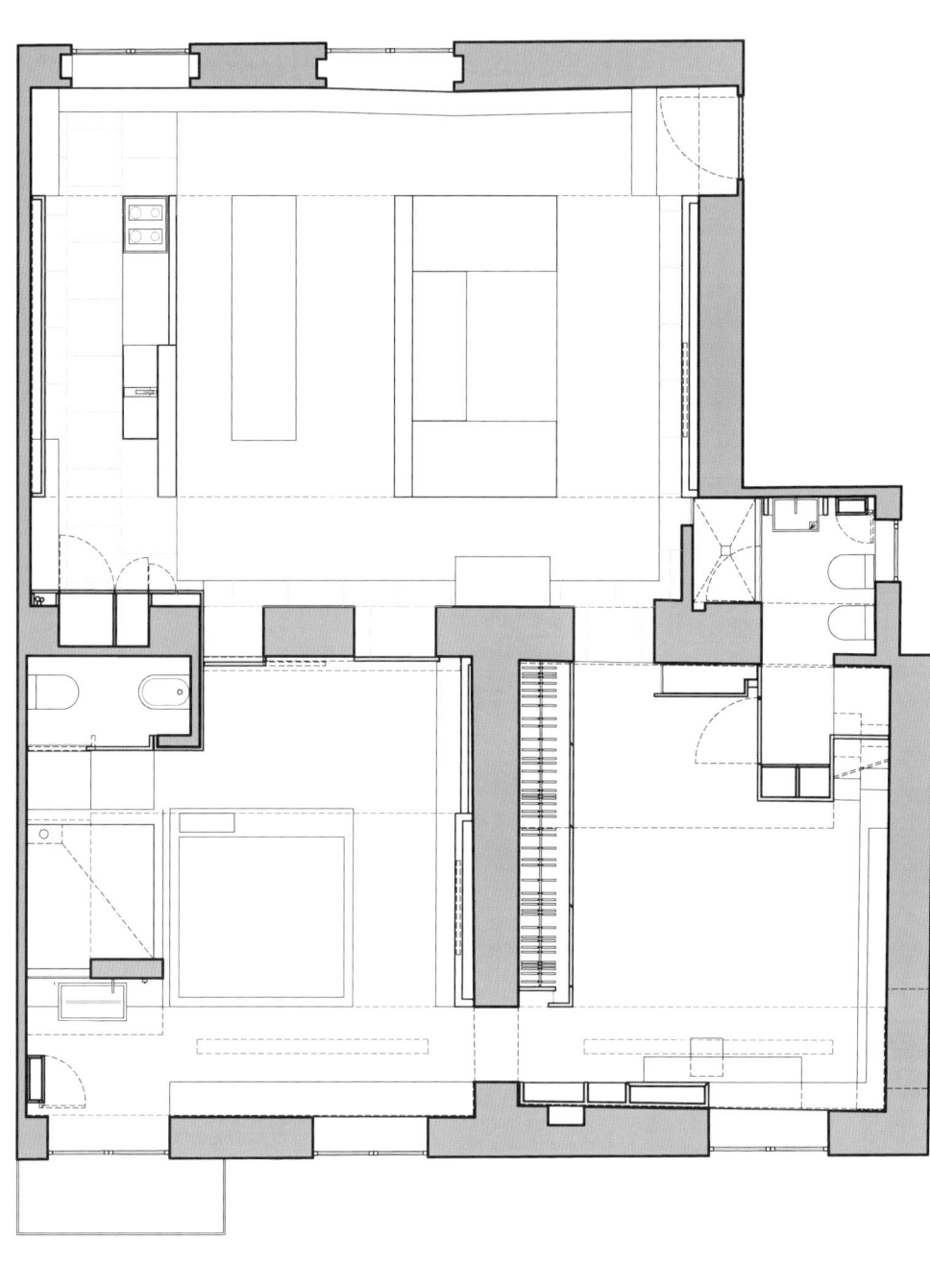

Floor

0   1   2

The apartment stands out for the precision and purity of its design, from the integration of the spaces to the subtle contrasts between finishes, furniture, and flooring such as Wengue parquet and stone.

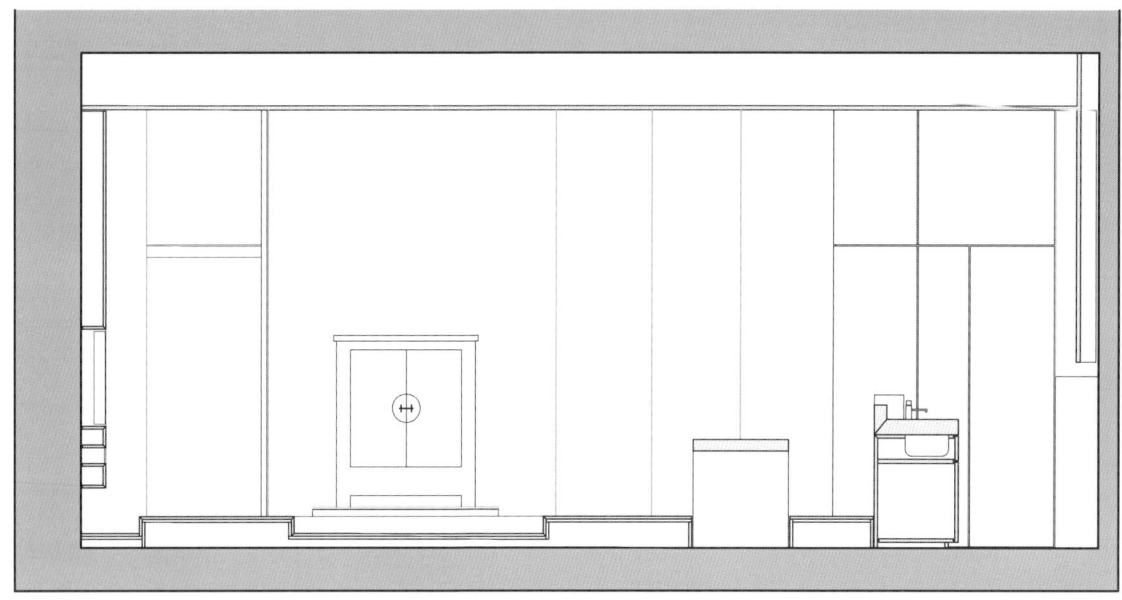

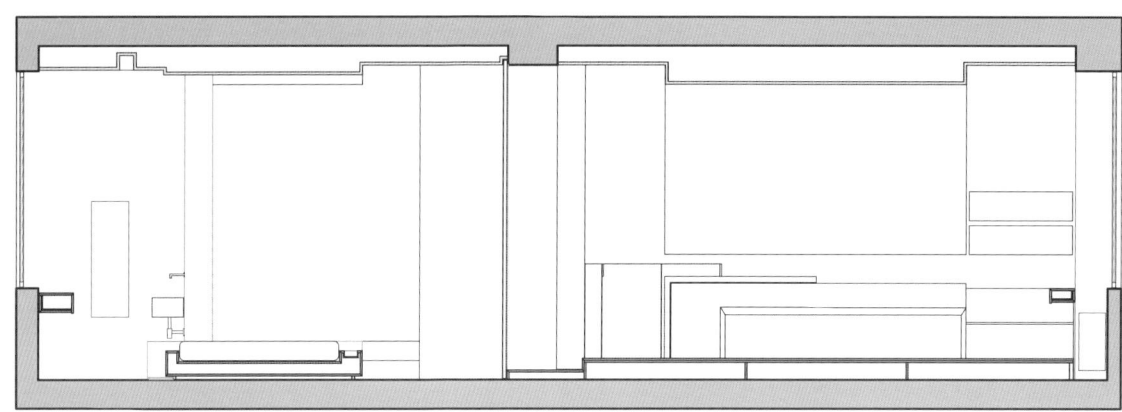

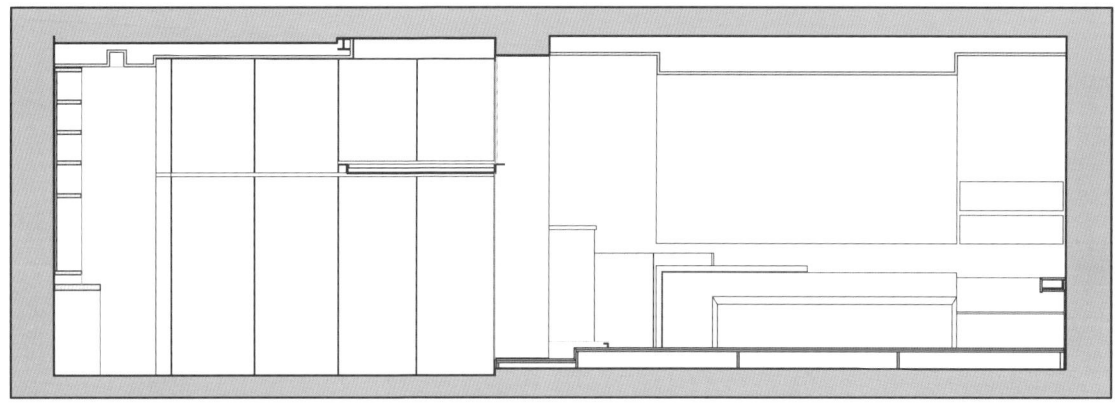

Longitudinal sections

Begur House

MARTA CERVELLÓ/MAP ARQUITECTOS

Despite being set in a rather rural setting, the strong urban and contemporary touches to this house more than justifies its appearance in this book.

The prospect includes a living space with three bedrooms and a guest apartment with independent entry. The building's shape is conceived from materials and minimal elements so as to heighten the spatial dimension and the entry of light. The unevenness of the site has been well utilized for the distribution of the house; the garage facing the street separates the main rooms in the two living areas and, by integrating the car, serves as a vestibule with a markedly contemporary air. The centre of the house is the main living area, being completely open with sliding doors leading to the porch and garden. The kitchen is a large independent module located between the staircase and the dining room, and it is perfectly integrated into the main bedroom. The finishes are simple and effective with chestnut wood and polished cement flooring, plaster walls and enamelled structural pillars.

Location: Girona, Spain I **Contributors:** María Viñé I **Completion Date:** 2004 I **Area:** 250 m² I **Photography:** Jordi Miralles

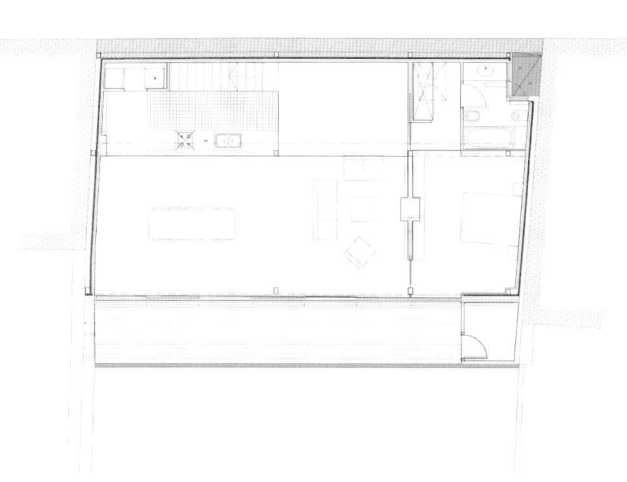

Ground floor

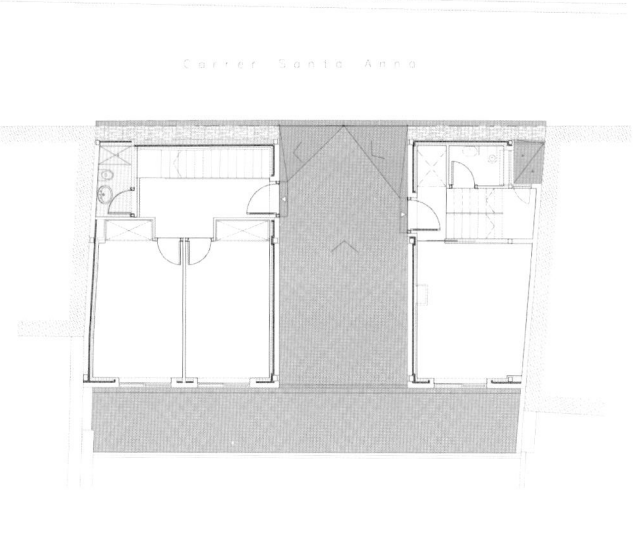

First floor

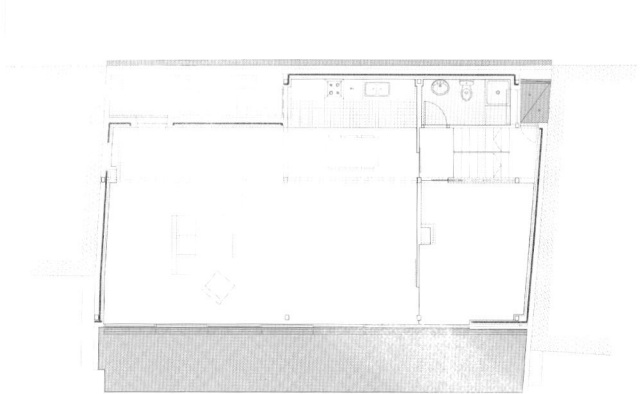

Second floor

Roof terrace plan

0   1   2

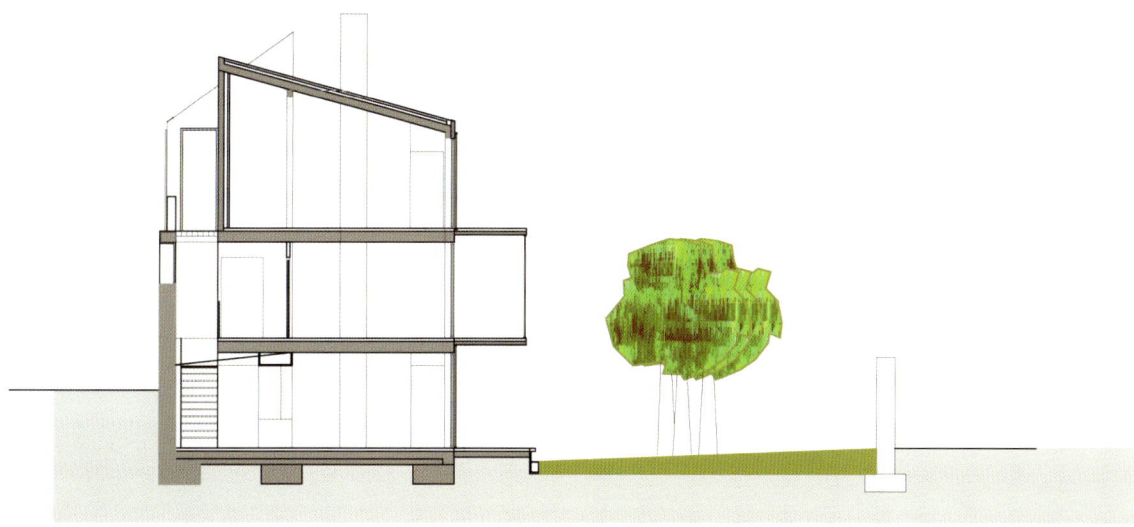

Longitudinal section

Cross section

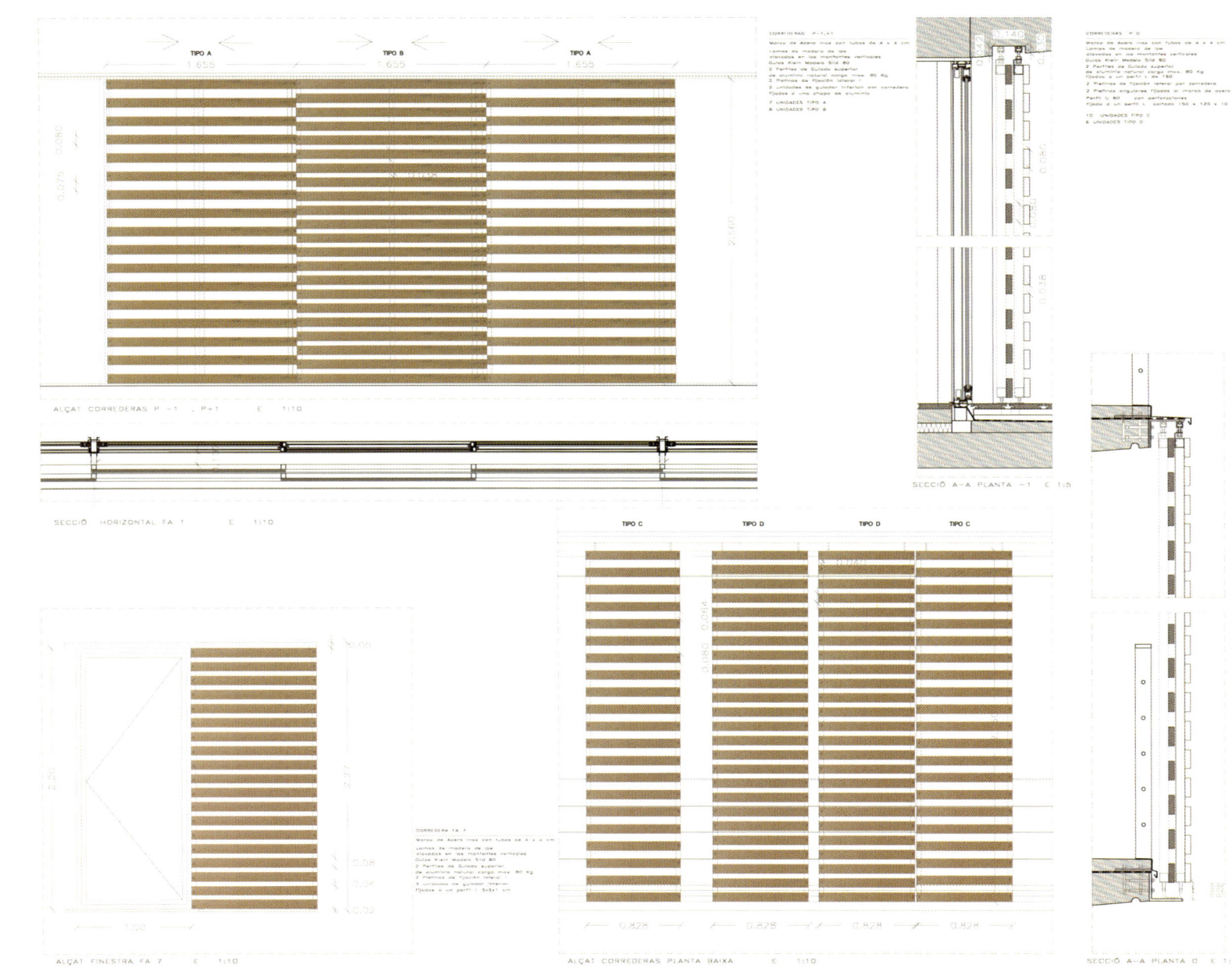

Facade detail

The sliding doors made of a metal frame
and ipe wood which diffuses the light
and lends continuity and dynamism to
the facade alongside the garden.

Perkins Herbert House

JENSEN & MACY ARCHITECTS

This San Francisco living space, highlighted by the use of unique elements within a normal proposal for a small family, occupies the top half of a small renovated building. It draws attention thanks to its unusual distribution –the bedrooms are on the lower level and the common areas are on the top level– done to take advantage of the city views and improve the lighting. In this way the second level becomes the main area in the living space, and it is highlighted by a kitchen island lined with Corian, forming the nucleus of the house and from which the rest of the rooms are organized.

A large white block holds one of the fundamental requirements of the clients: a mixing table built into the kitchen which acts as a DJ booth. This functional duality is extended throughout the main level, as during the day it is a generously lit space and by night, a discothèque.

A large overhead skylight fills the upper floor with light which reaches the lower bedrooms through a double glass floor. At the same time, a polycarbonate wall filters light into the staircase and giving it clarity and transparency.

Location: San Francisco, California, USA | **Completion Date:** 2001 | **Area:** 138 m² | **Photography:** Roger Casas

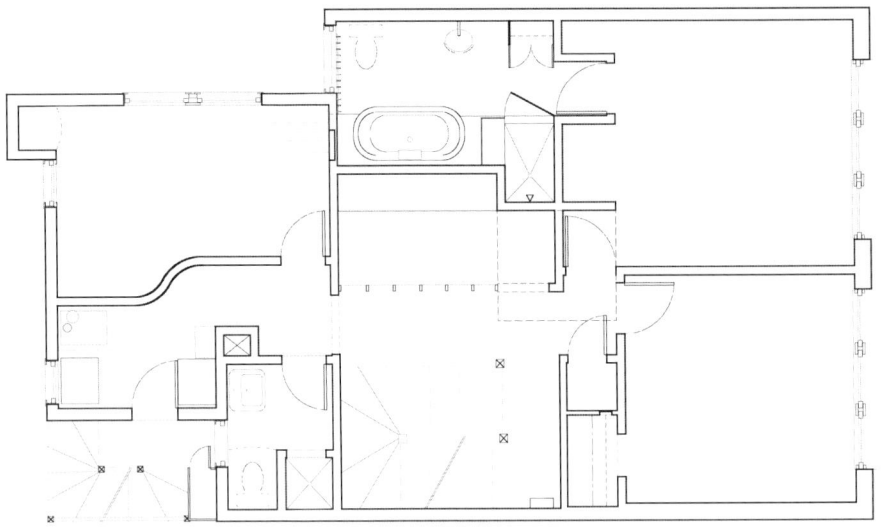

Lower level

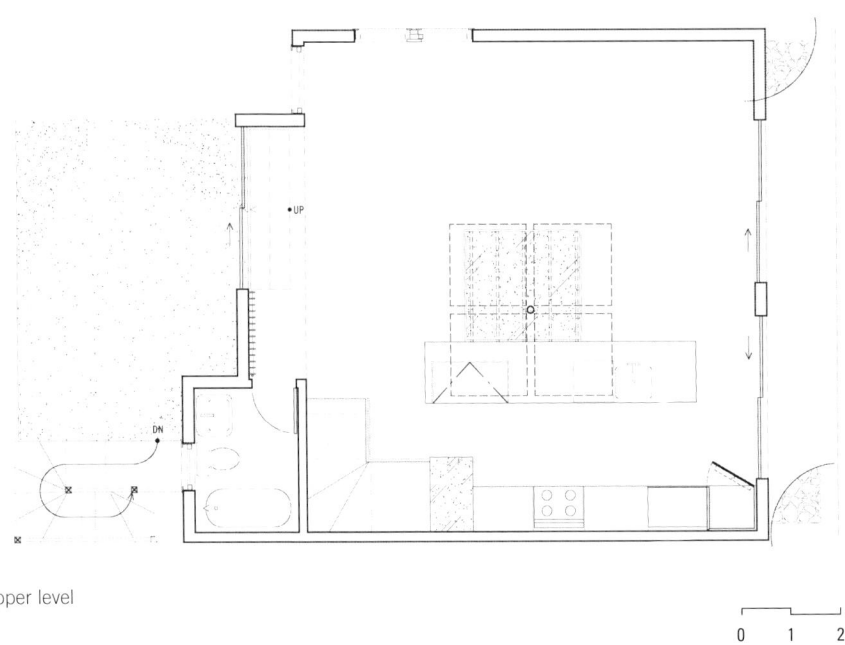

Upper level

0 1 2

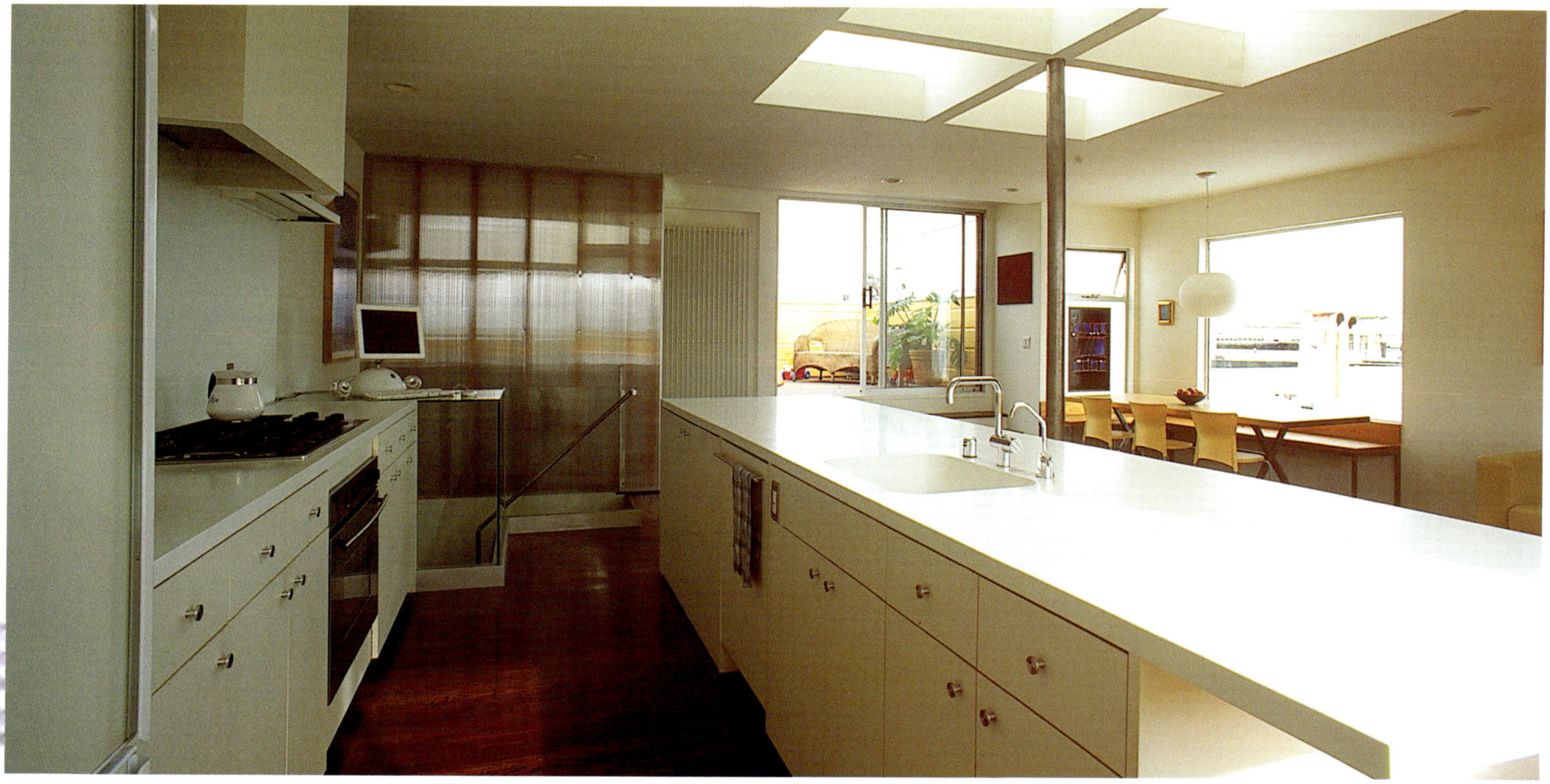

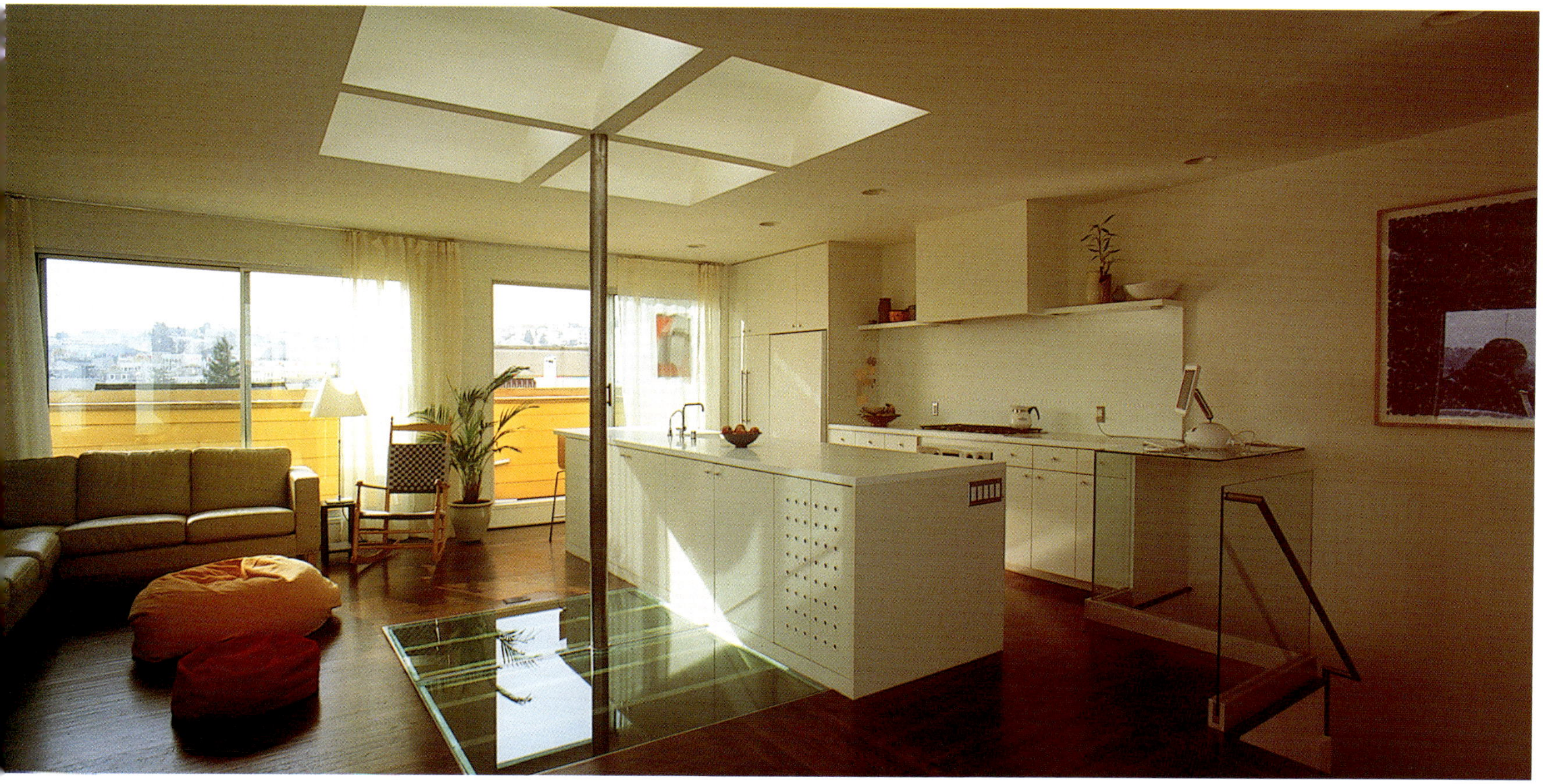

Kang Duplex

SHI-CHIEH LU/CJ STUDIO

This project consists in the renovation of a duplex located on a bustling street in the centre of Taipei. As this is a party wall building, the surface area is long and narrow and there is sparse lighting. To solve this, the rear facade has been replaced with frosted glass and all the walls, floors and ceiling have been painted white to lend continuity to the project and structure the space's interior which is inspired by origami.

A two-floor open space vertically unites the studio and living area and is the central nucleus of the living space. Likewise, the two floors are connected by a polished methacrylate staircase next to the street facade. The staircase starts at the bottom of a window and rises to the living area and its transparent steps capture light and dynamically filter it towards the interior. At the opposite end, the original staircase joining the bedroom and the kitchen has been kept in order to lend fluidity; in this way, the entire space of the duplex can be seen as a loop in constant motion.

Location: Taipei, Taiwan | **Contributors:** Black Wu | **Completion Date:** 2001 | **Area:** 130 m² | **Photography:** Kuomin Lee

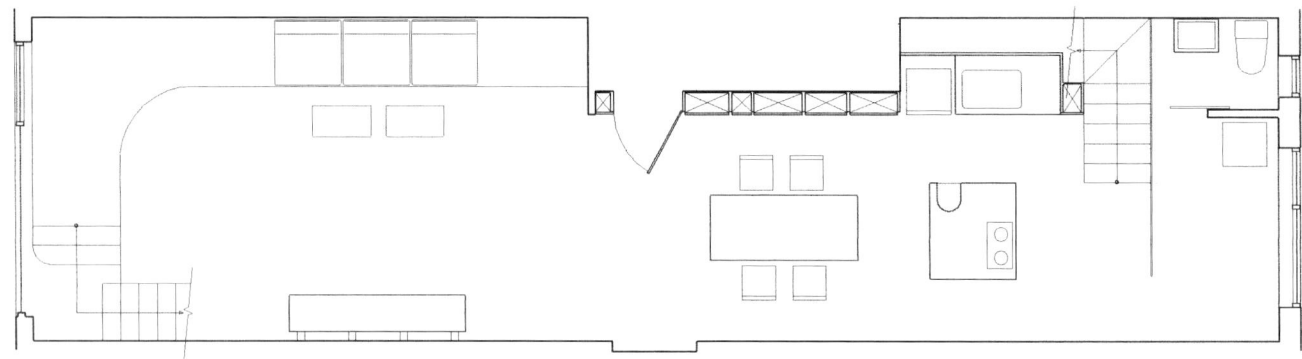

Lower level

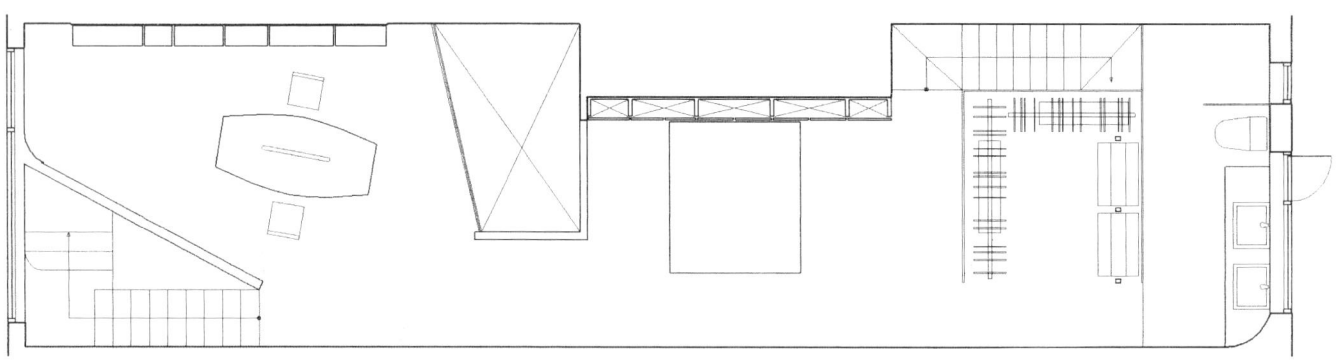

Upper level

0   1   2

The entrance forms a convex volume
which makes the space even
narrower and this is lined with
wardrobes covered in turquoise
methacrylate to produce a slight
contrast with the dominant whiteness
and feeling of lightness.

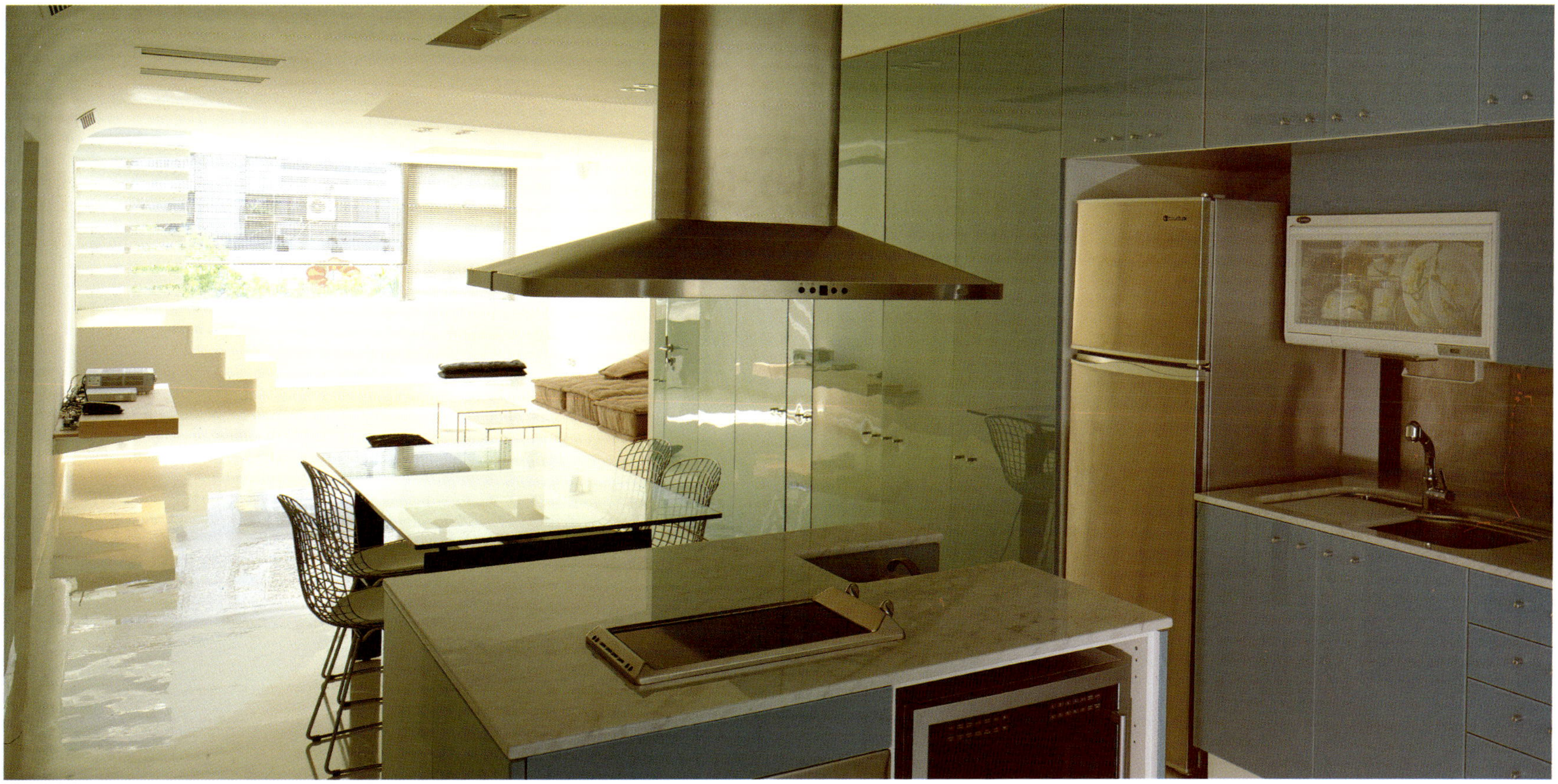

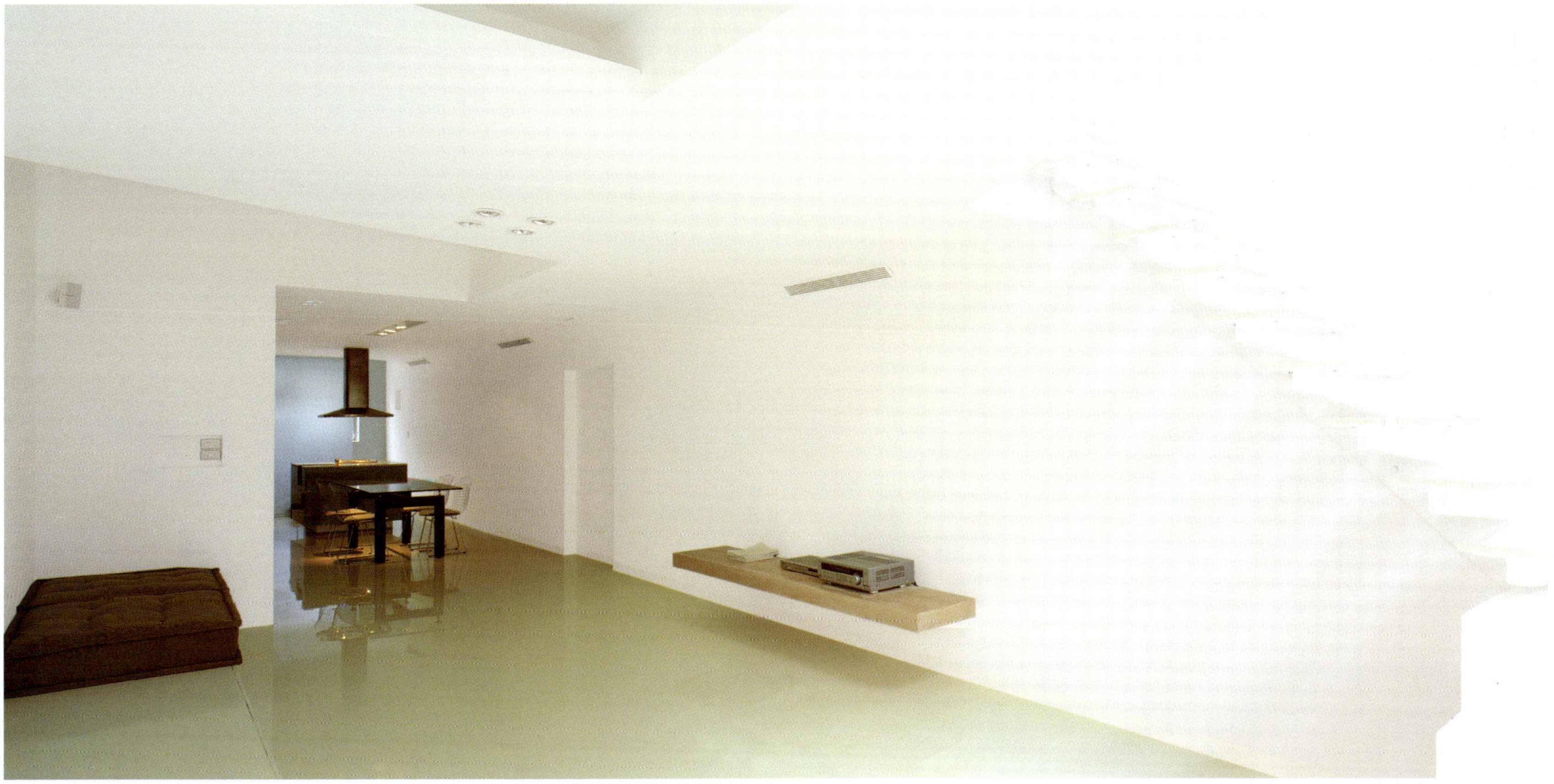

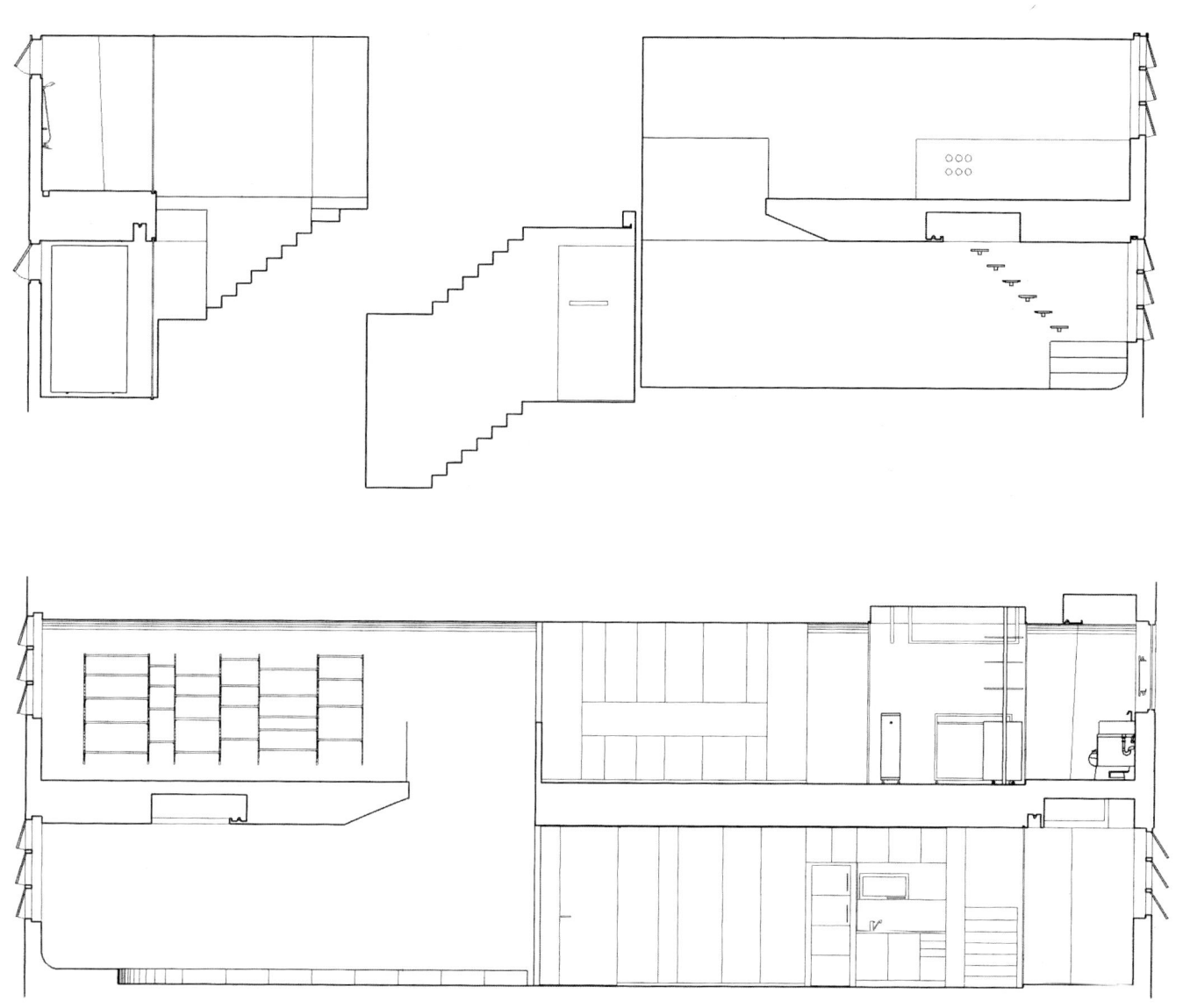

Longitudinal sections

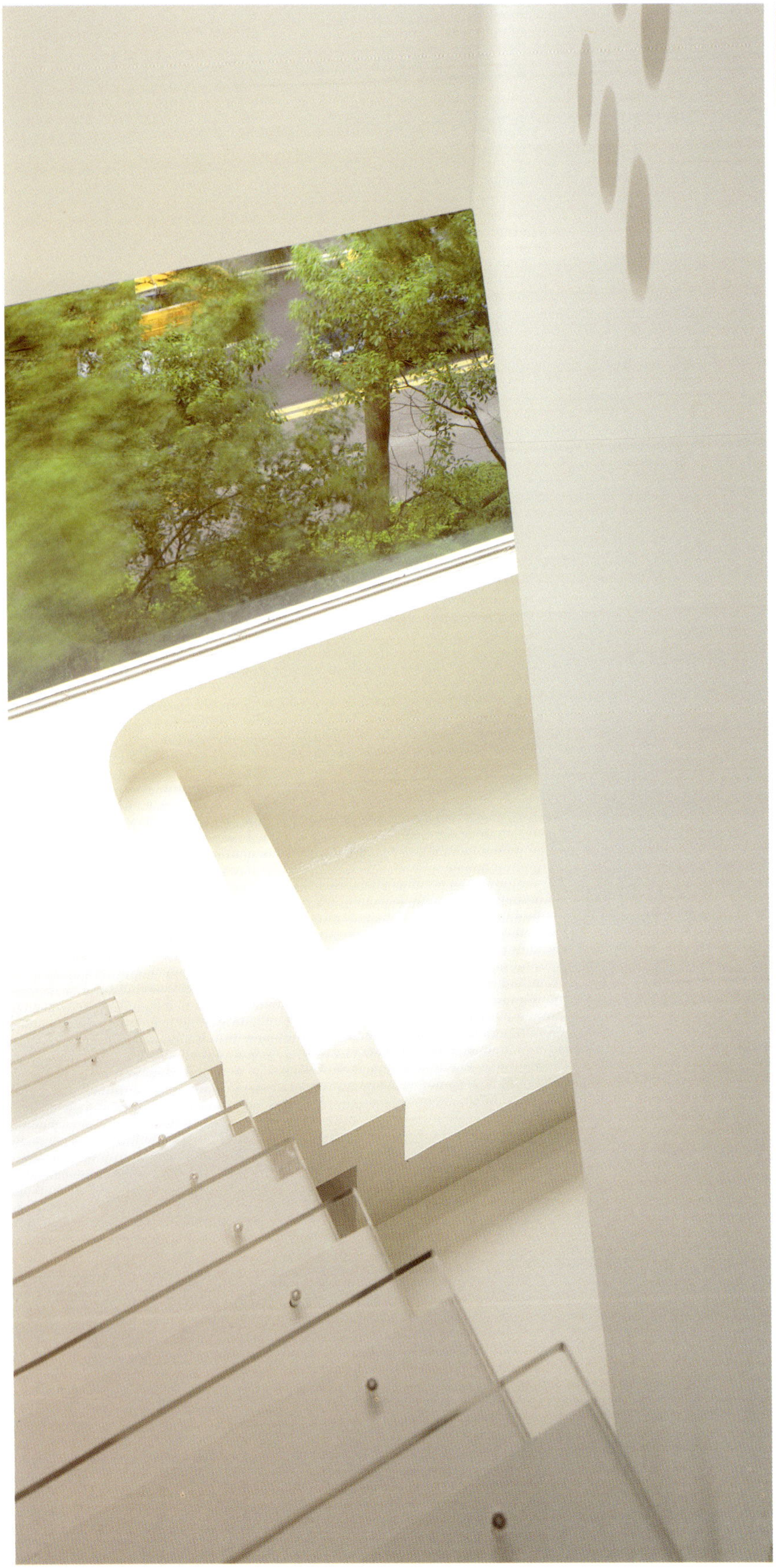

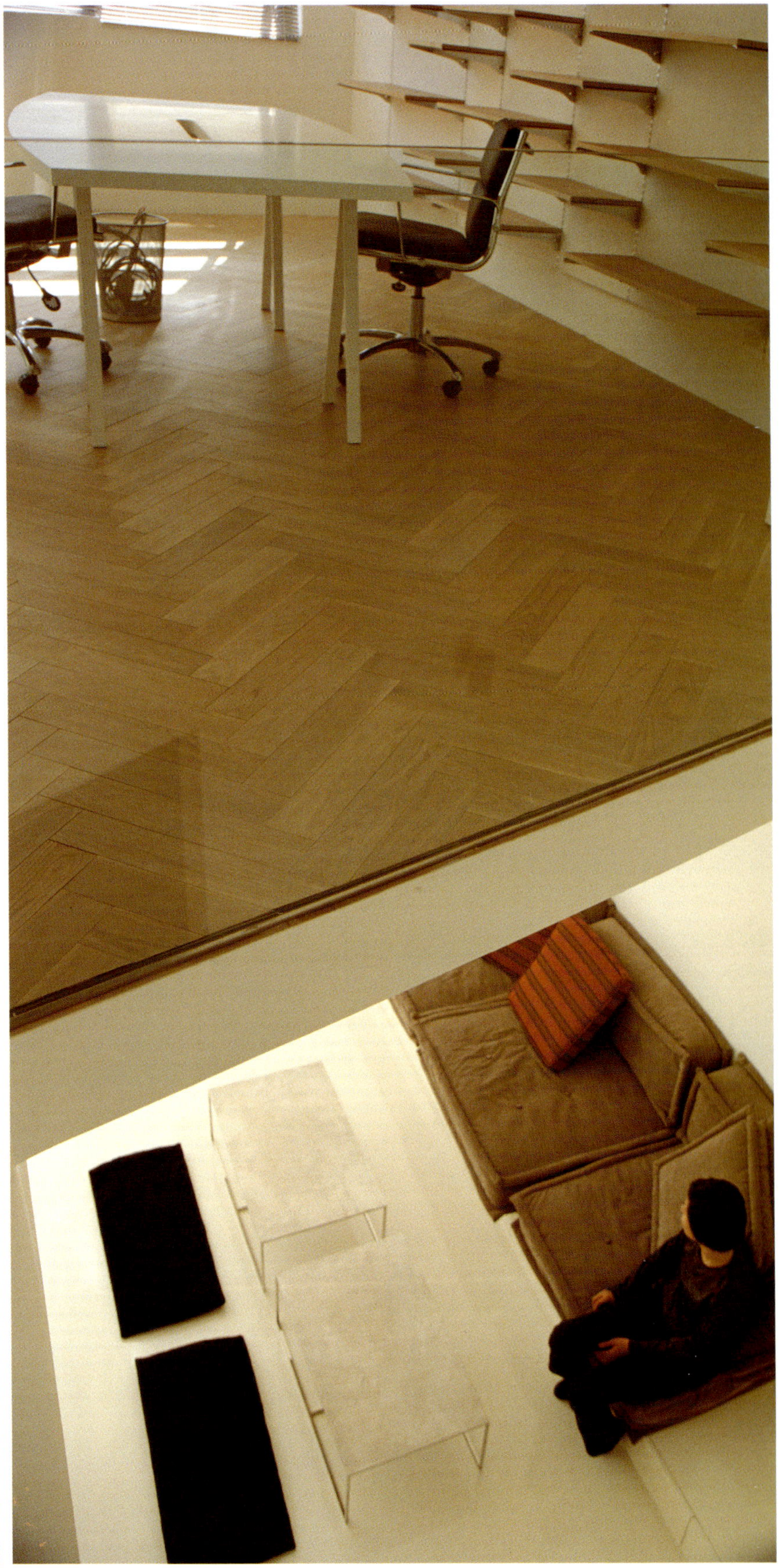

Xiangshan Apartment

HANK M. CHAO/MOHEN INTERNATIONAL

Located in the heart of Shanghai, a city whose interiors tend to be poorly done copies of Western values, this apartment stands out for both its Oriental and enduring elegance. The project answered the wishes of the owner to create a refuge set within which would use different textures and materials and where dark tones would predominate. Uncut grey granite and stainless steel panels, rusted metal and corten steel define the apartment's interior finishes.

From the entrance, a rough metal wall acting as wardrobe invites one inside; the private space here is separated from the public by an interior bamboo garden that is dramatically illuminated from the floor and seen from the entrance. The dining room table stands out in the main area, a floating panel of extruded steel with a water vessel at each end that hides its structure. The bedroom, with warmer tones and wood flooring, has a large pivoting rusted door to define its space.

Location: Shanghai, China I **Completion Date:** 2004 I **Area:** 180 m² I **Photography:** Maoder Chou

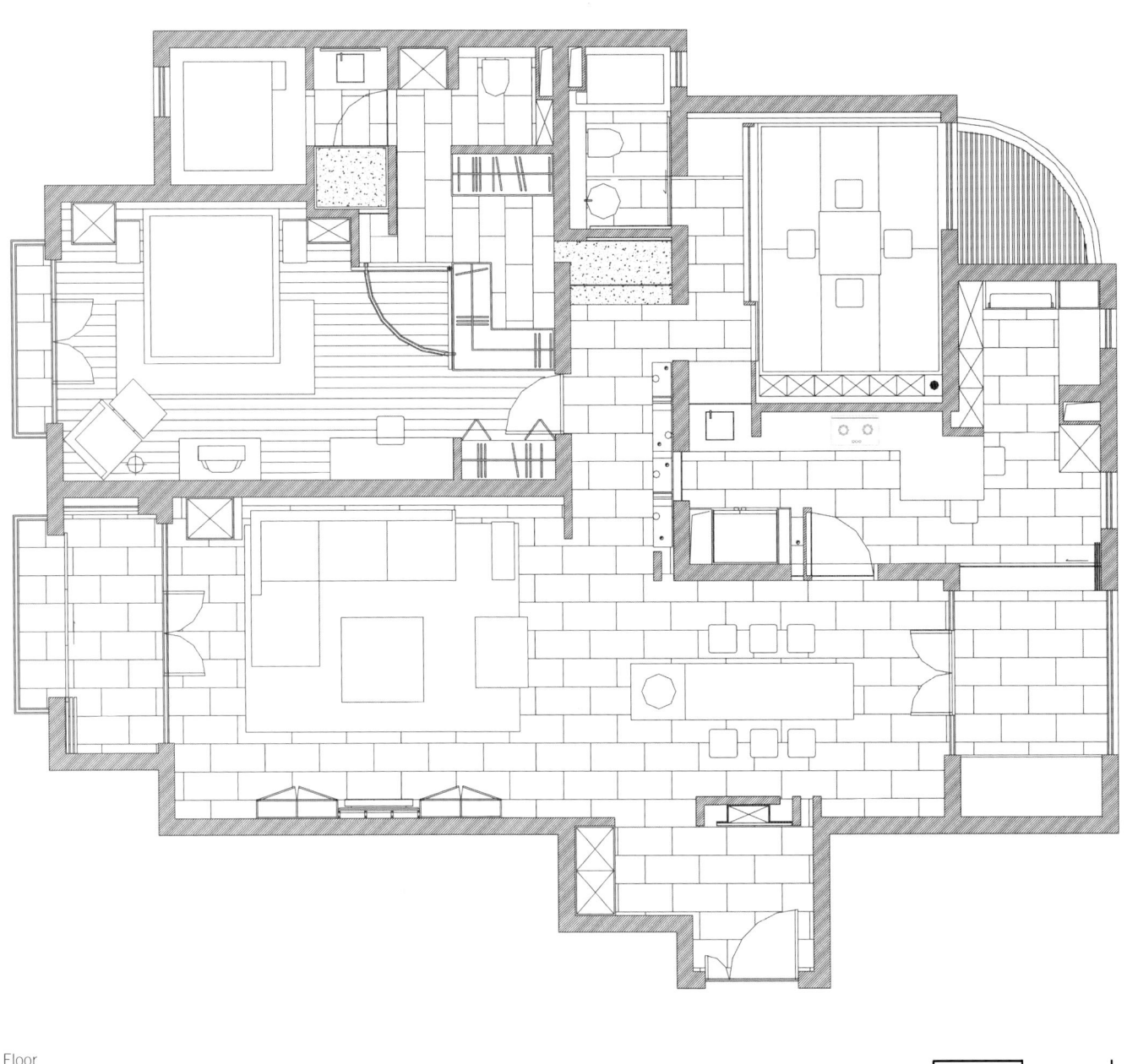

Floor

0   1   2

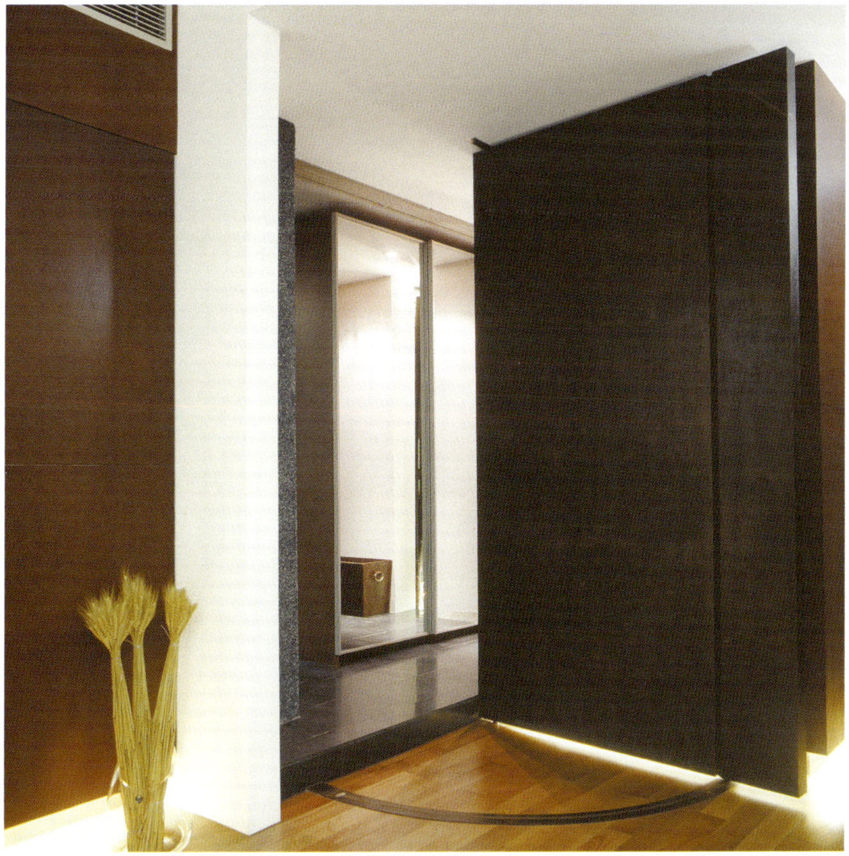

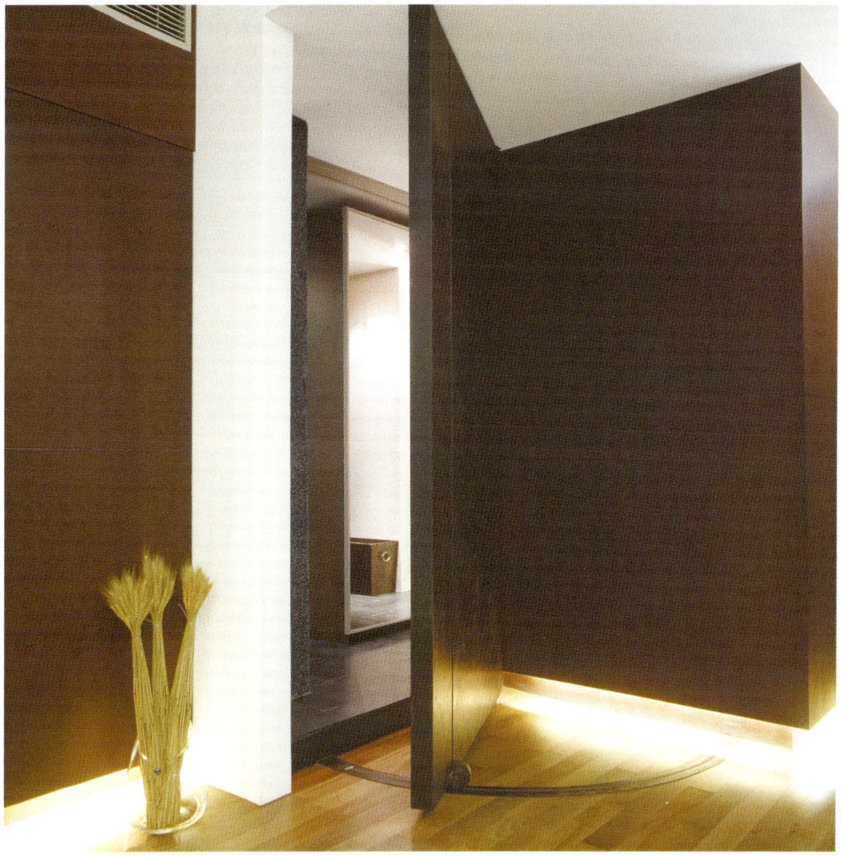

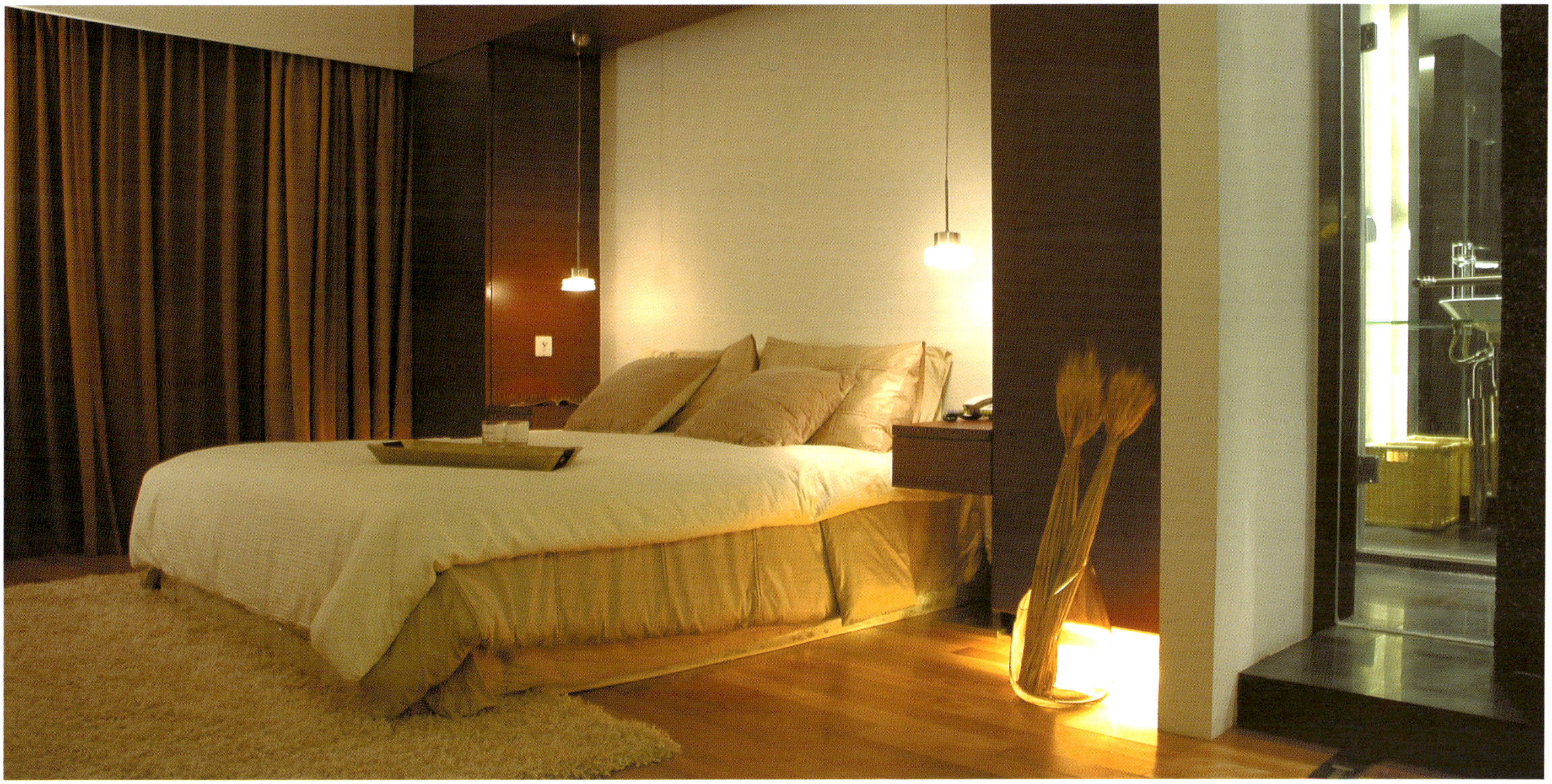

Frankfurt Penthouse Flat

HOLLIN RADOSKE ARCHITEKTEN

Located in an impressive modern 1954 building, this penthouse is a magnificent example of a renovation blending into the context in which it is found. The interior is completely new; only the yellow bricks on the three perimeter dummy walls remain from the previous penthouse. A terrace runs entirely around the flat offering magnificent views of the city. The living space is distributed around two open patios which fill the interior with overhead light: one of them is surrounded by a bamboo garden and has a large hydro-massage and shower for summertime; the other is a contemplative space, from a clearly Oriental inspiration, with wood deck and gold fish pond.

The central nucleus of the house is the kitchen, with a rough slate surface which extends into the dining area and dies off in the living room, bringing fluidity to all three.

The guest bedroom has a separate entrance and is designed to obtain the most flexibility possible, as all the bedrooms can be connected or divided among themselves.

Location: Frankfurt, Germany | **Completion Date:** 2005 | **Area:** 135 m² | **Photography:** Ludger Paffrath

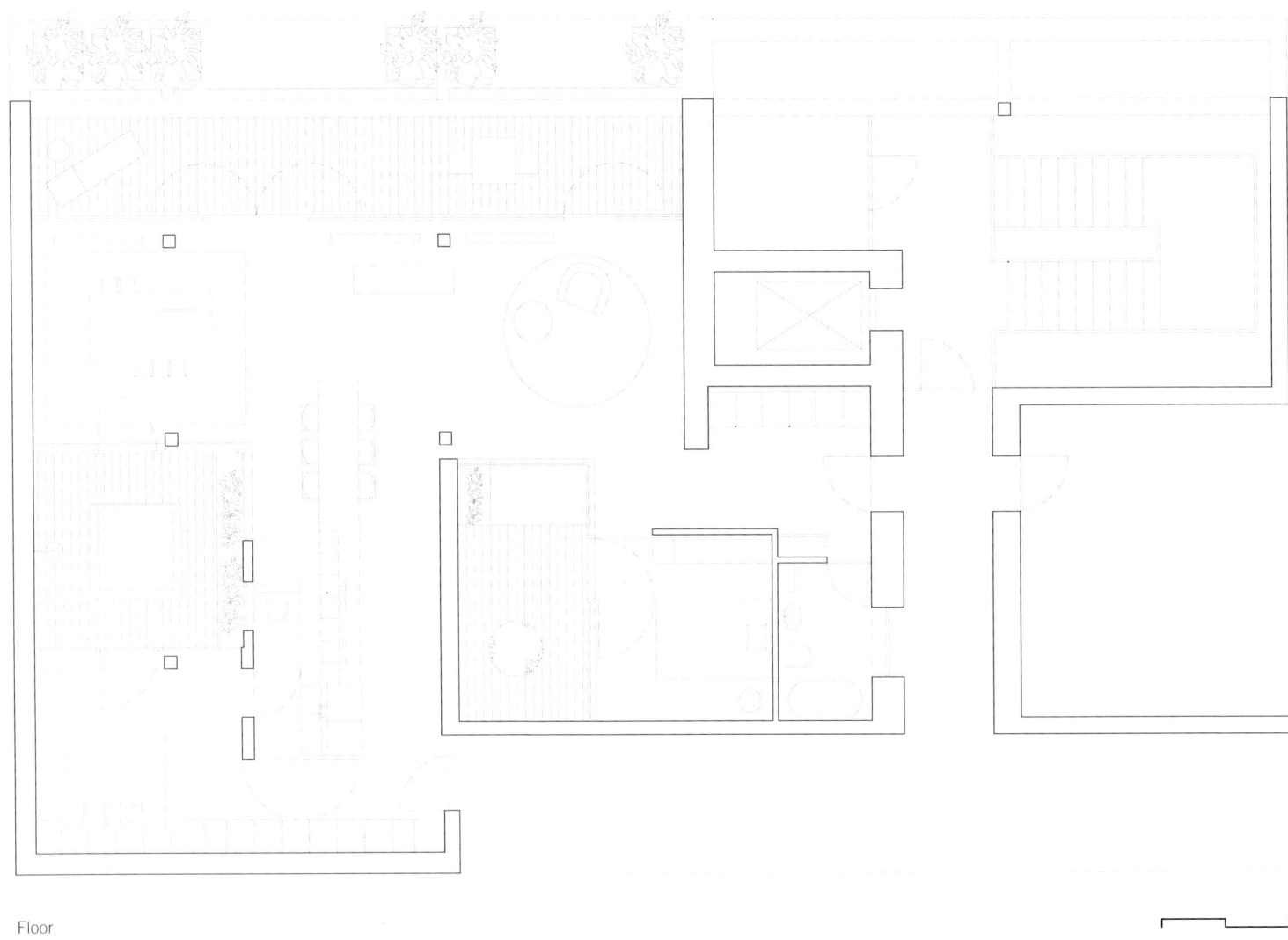

Floor

0   1   2

Both the low central table and the sideboard with built-in lighting were designed by the architects.

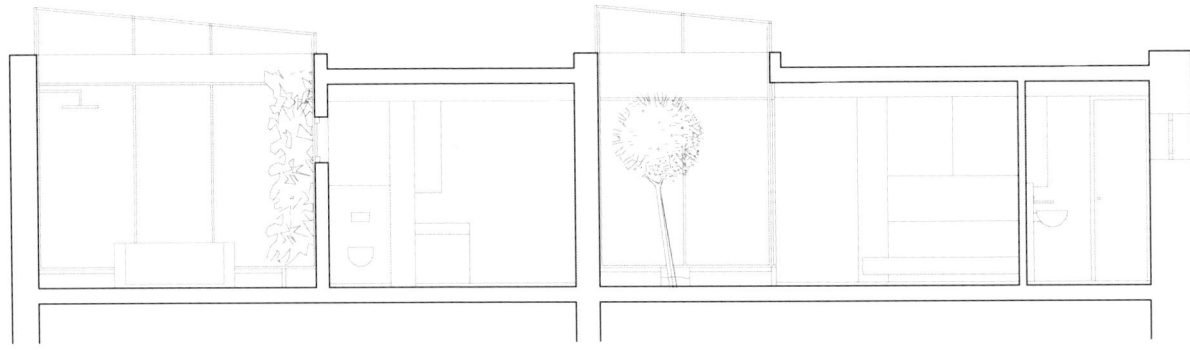

Longitudinal section

Cross section

The interior is highlighted by the
special attention paid to detail; for
example, a complete "home cinema"
including projector, screen and
speakers has been remarkably
hidden in the ceiling.

Sullivan Street Loft

TINA MANIS ASSOCIATES LLC

Located in Soho, the design of this loft is derived from a programme that examines the transition from public spaces to private ones. Apart from this main proposal, the living space is divided into three areas separated by just three large moving panels which maintain the spatial ambiguity and flexibility typical of a loft.

In this rather linear way, the intimate area of the bedroom flows into the entertainment area of the living room by way of the kitchen: a multipurpose area that serves as both a dining room and an informal gathering area. This is the most dynamic and open area of the apartment, being illuminated overhead by a large skylight and windows which look out over the urban landscape. The remaining service areas are located next to the kitchen: a wash basin interconnected to the main bathroom offers an ingenious and practical solution to one of the desires of the owner to have two complete baths while sustaining the concept of flexibility that defines the project.

Location: New York, New York, USA | **Completion Date.** 2004 | **Area:** 230 m² | **Photography:** Rjorg Magnea

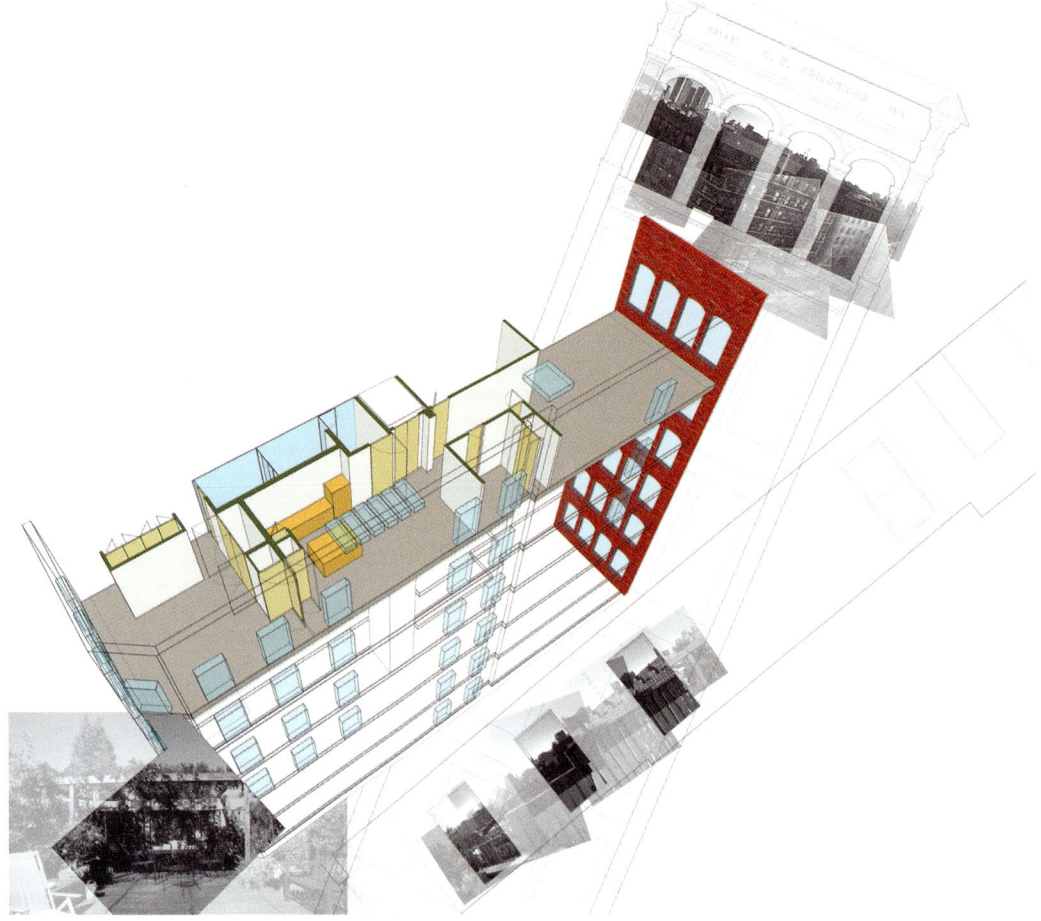

Perspective

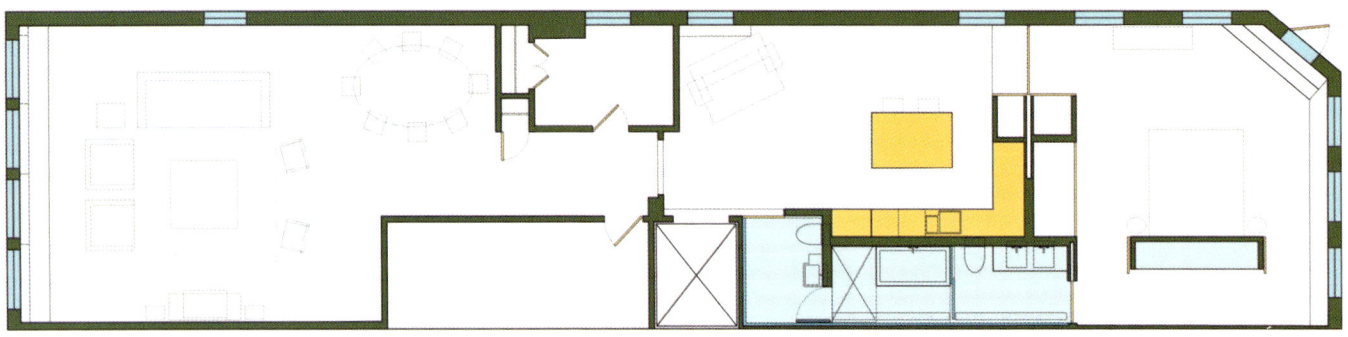

Floor

0 1 2

Piazza Navona House

ROBERTO SILVESTRI/SILVESTRI ARCHITETTURA

Located in the heart of the Italian capital, this apartment belongs to a film director. The architect remained in close contact with the client during the renovation process so that the result would match his tastes and personality; in this way, the plan for the living space would respect the ideas and wishes of its occupant.

The main element of the transformation can be seen from the entrance: a dark rough wall running perpendicular to the length of the apartment. Along with a second wall, this one lined with Corten steel, both form a cube enclosing a studio separated by two sliding glass walls which can be made into a guest bedroom. This material defines the interior space; it establishes an interesting dialogue with the parquet and strong contrast with the white walls. To strengthen the common areas, both the service areas as well as the private areas are quite small, nearly minimal. Next to the kitchen, which is open to the rest of the house, a broad terrace extends out over the square and Roman rooftops.

Location: Rome, Italy | **Contributors:** Maria Previti | **Completion Date:** 2002 | **Area:** 110 m² | **Photography:** Ernesta Caviola

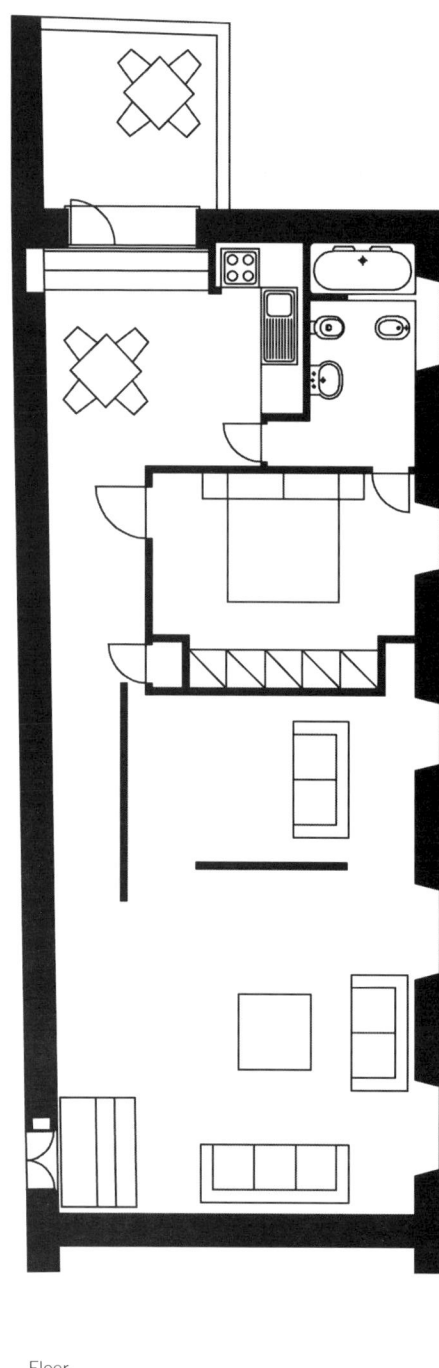

Floor

0   1   2

The interior, conceived as a
longitudinal succession of areas,
becomes completely defined by the
two walls lined with three-millimetre
corten steel plates.

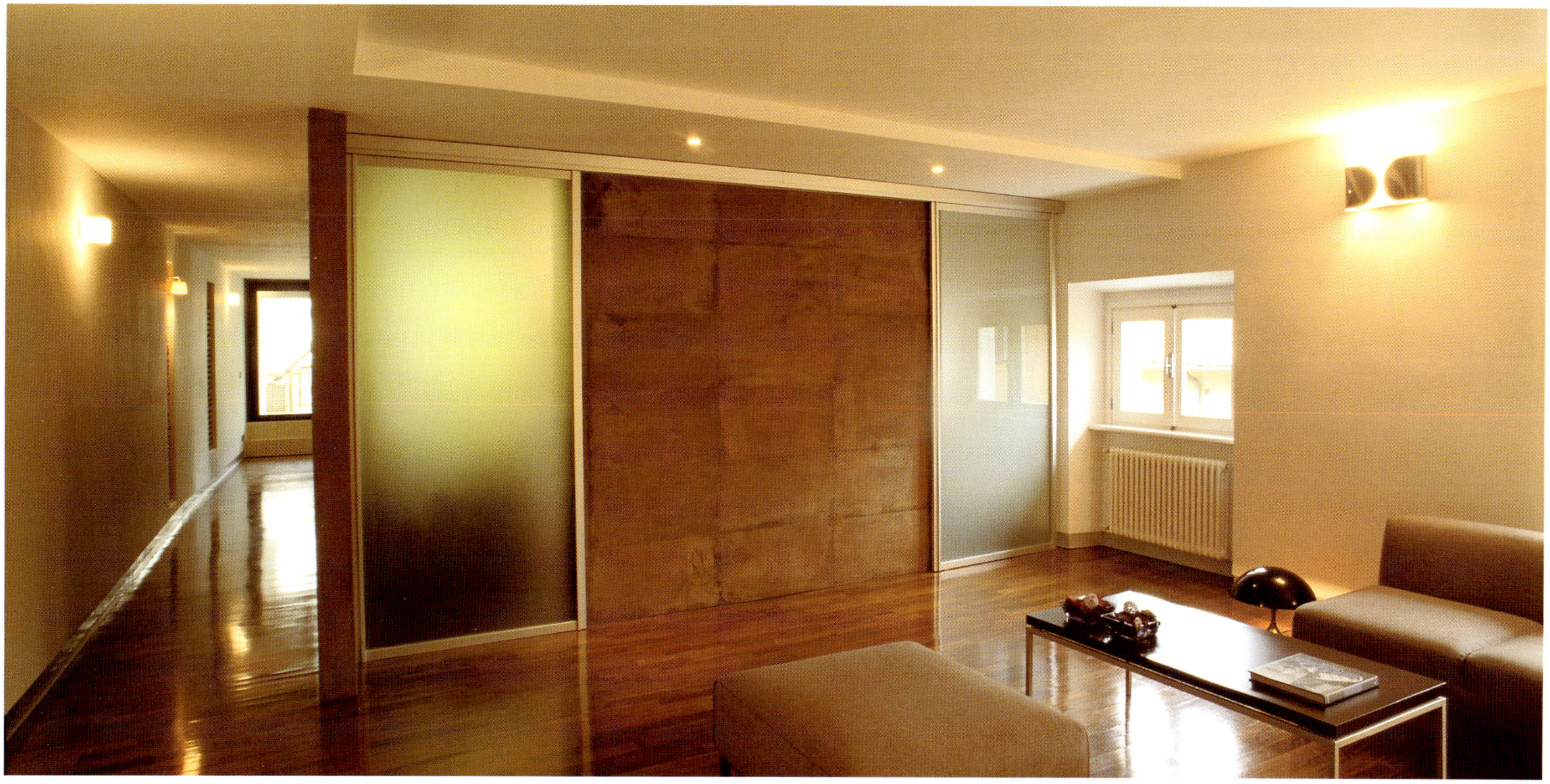

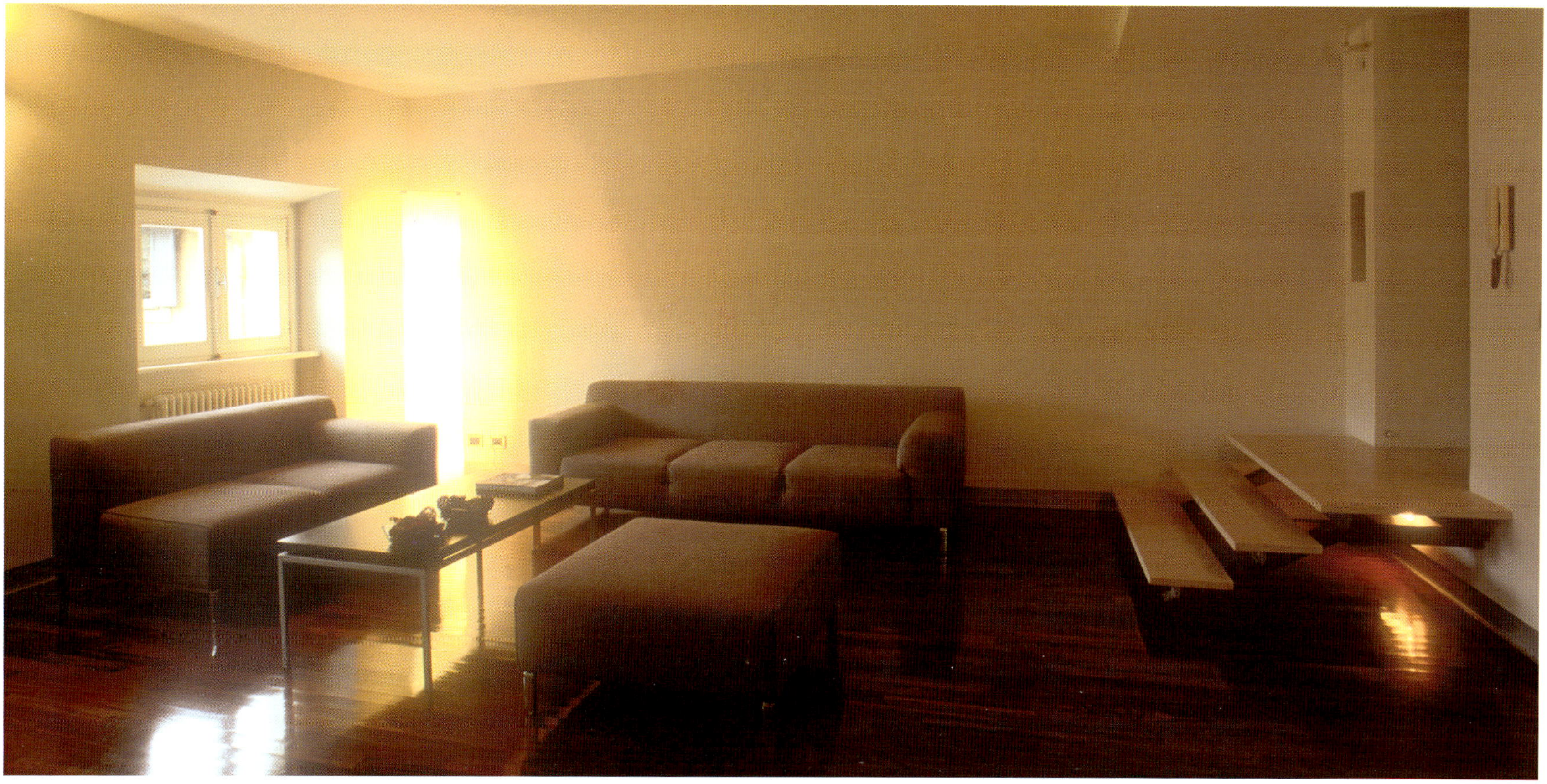

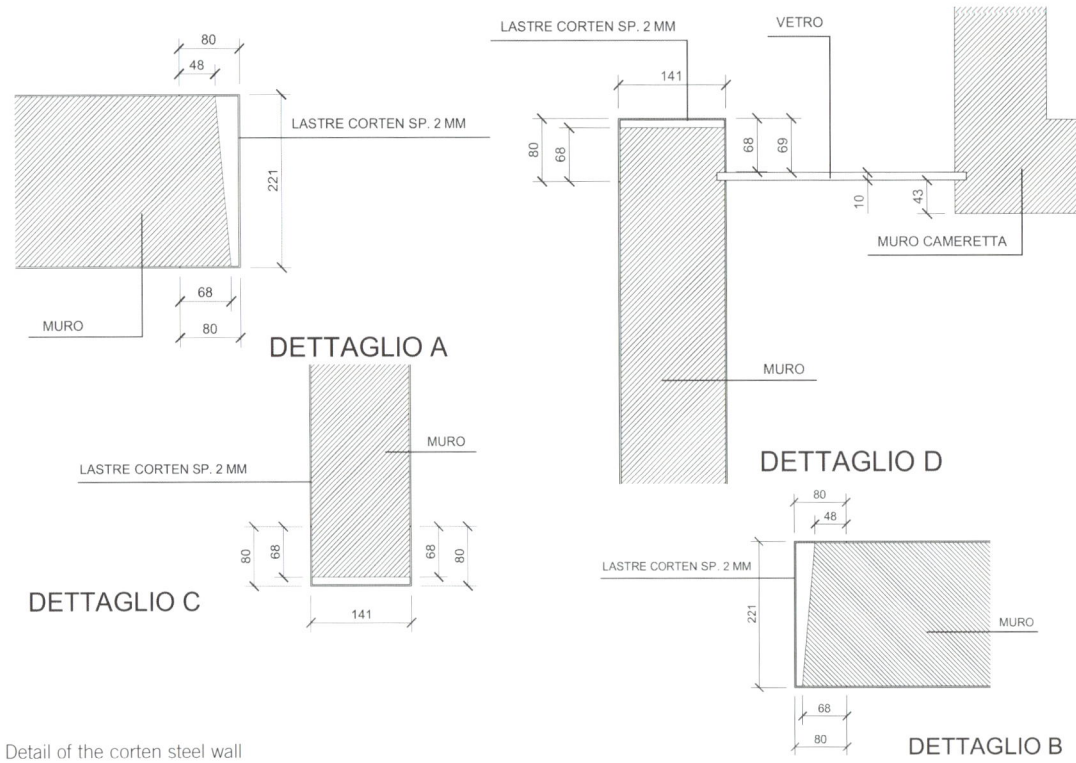

80
48
221
LASTRE CORTEN SP. 2 MM

MURO
68
80

DETTAGLIO A

LASTRE CORTEN SP. 2 MM
MURO
80 68
68 80
141

DETTAGLIO C

LASTRE CORTEN SP. 2 MM
VETRO
141
80 68
68 69
10 43

MURO CAMERETTA
MURO

DETTAGLIO D

80
48
LASTRE CORTEN SP. 2 MM
221
MURO
68
80

DETTAGLIO B

Detail of the corten steel wall

Choy House

CARY BERNSTEIN

This project consisted of a complete renovation of a small Victorian house from 1908 which included the construction of an addition floor. By adding a glassed-in extension to the street facade, the distributing hallway became a broad light-filled vestibule. The relationship established between this element and the metal staircase leading to the upper floor permitted the traditional superimposition of floors to be transformed into an interconnected and dynamic space. For its part, the new facade demonstrates a restrained conciliation with the former building and a newer open and contemporary aesthetic.

In the ample living area occupying the first floor, the balanced integration of the kitchen and the dining room truly stands out, along with the fireplace as its main feature with its large steel-plated armature stretching from ceiling to floor in counterpoint to the staircase.

The second floor houses the bedroom and the main bathroom with some large window walls that completely launch the space outward to the exterior. The continuity of the dampened organic tones throughout the living space accentuates the space, light and magnificent views of the city.

Location: San Francisco, California, USA I **Completion Date:** 2002 I **Area:** 158 m² I **Photographer:** Roger Casas

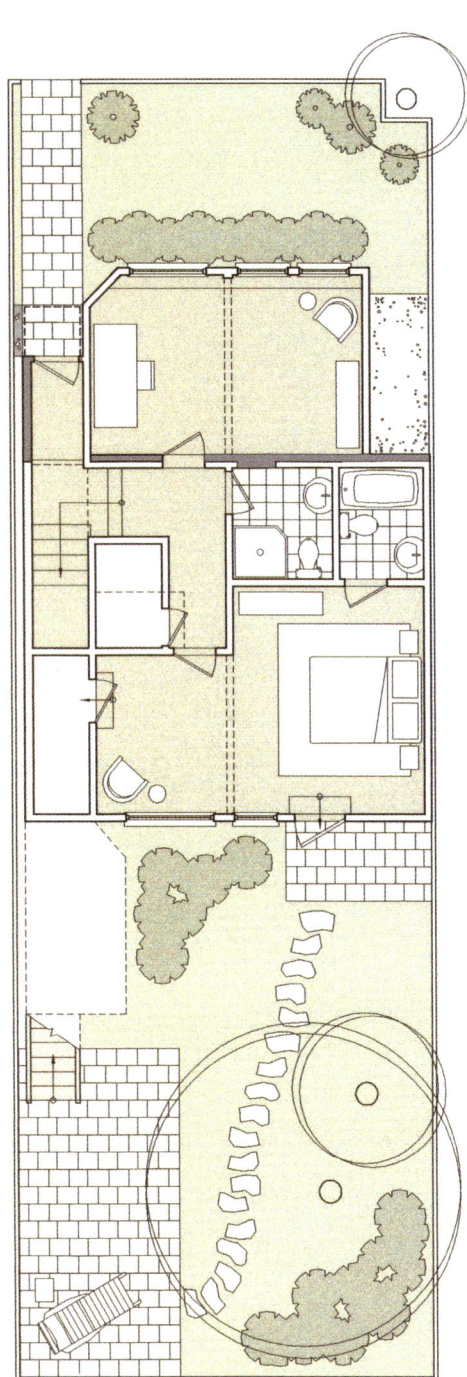

Ground floor

First floor

Second floor

0   1   2

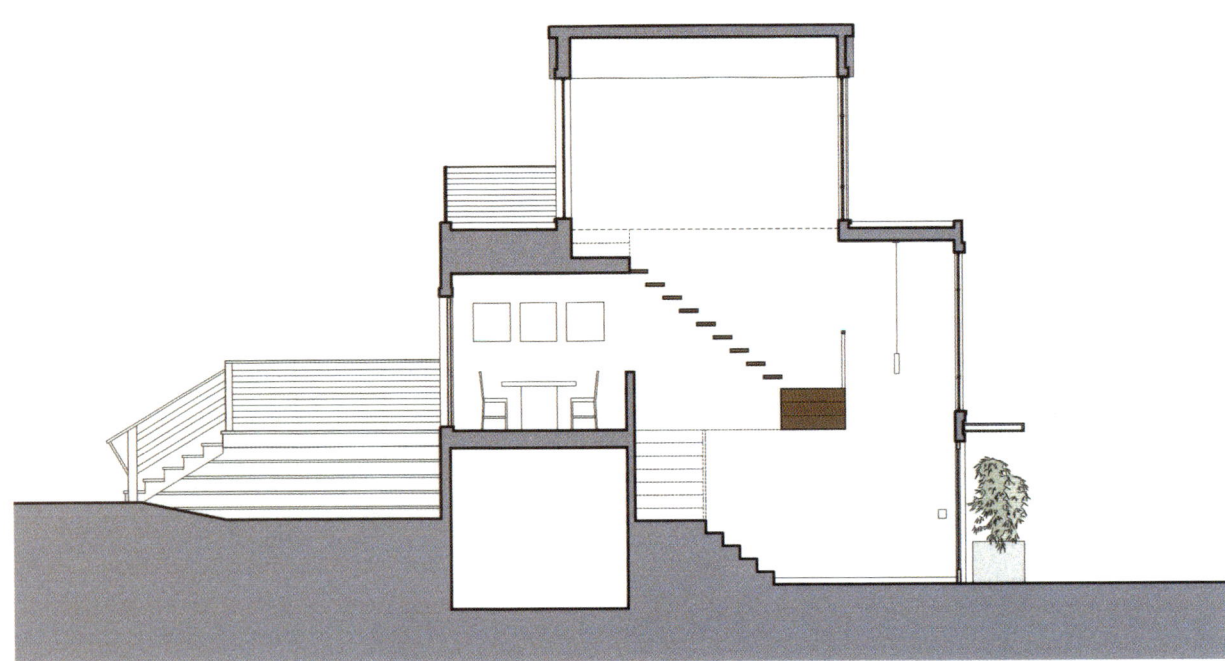

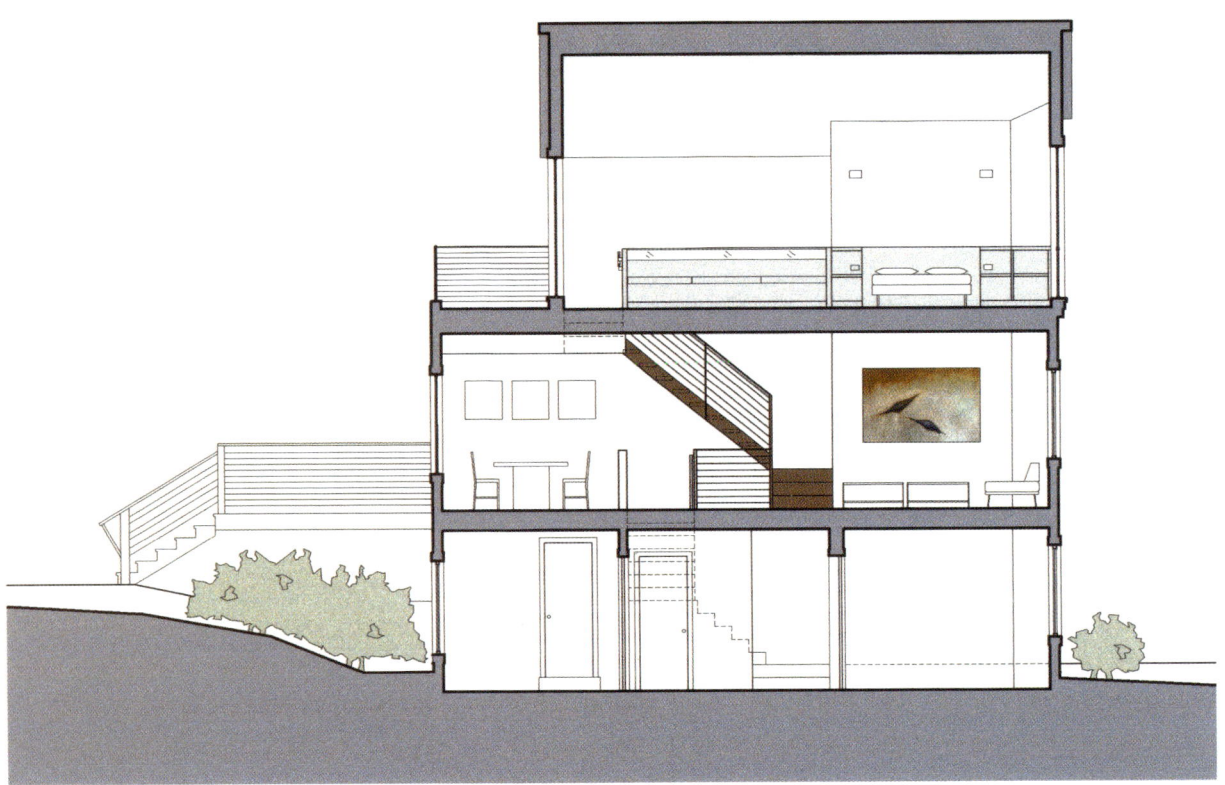

Longitudinal sections

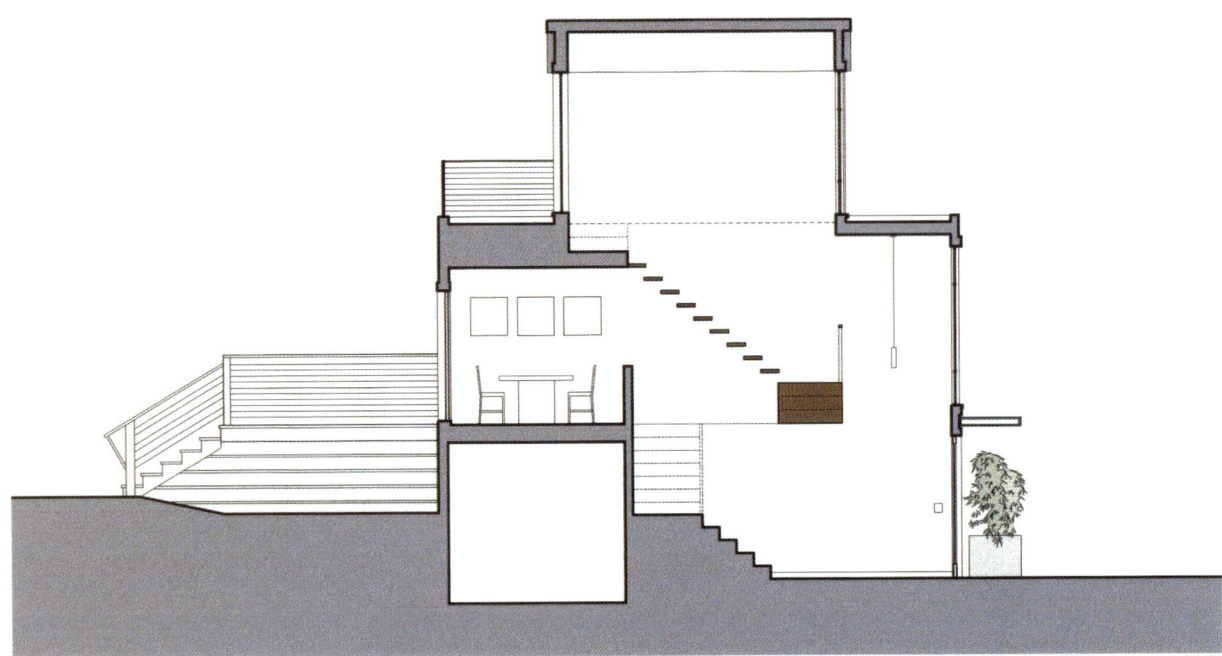

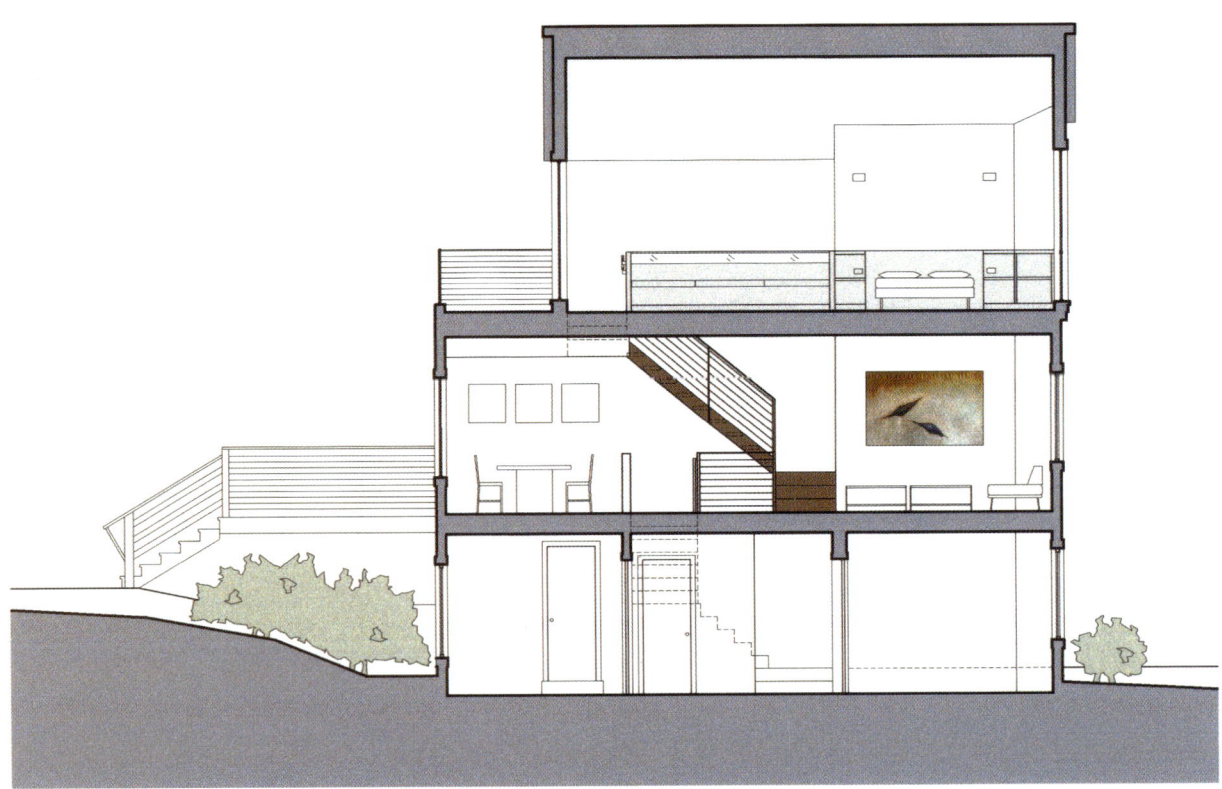

Longitudinal sections